A GEORGIA NATIVE PLANT GUIDE

A
GEORGIA
NATIVE ❀ PLANT
GUIDE

TINA M. SAMUELS

Mercer University Press | Macon, Georgia

ISBN 0-86554-878-1
MUP/P319

© 2005 Mercer University Press
1400 Coleman Avenue
Macon, Georgia 31207

First Edition

Book design by Burt and Burt Studio

Library of Congress Cataloging-in-Publication Data

Samuels, Tina M.
A Georgia native plant guide / Tina M. Samuels—1st ed.
p. cm.
Includes bibliographical references (p.   ) and index.
ISBN-13: 978-0-86554-878-7 (pbk.: alk. paper)
ISBN-10: 0-86554-878-1 (pbk.: alk. paper)
1. Native plants for cultivation—Georgia
2. Native plant
gardening—Georgia. I. Title.
SB439.24.G4S26 2005
635.9'51758—dc22

2005020722

CONTENTS

ACKNOWLEDGMENTS

I'd like to thank the experts and volunteers who were instrumental in making sure my train stayed on track. I'd also like to thank the people who made a personal touch. Any mistakes in this manuscript are my own fault, not that of the experts. They guided me along a path, but I may have stumbled on a few of the steps. I'm sure I'll forget to include someone or some organization, but please realize that if you don't see your name here, it's due to my own lapse of memory.

Thank you to Marc Jolley, the man who said "yes" at Mercer University Press; Kay Stephenson at Georgia Native Plant Society; Jennifer Ceska at the State Botanical Garden of Georgia; Carol Helton Denhof at the Atlanta Botanical Garden; Sue Brogdon at the Georgia Southern Botanical Garden; Kathie Weigel and Luke Cossins for their great Kudzu song; Carol Schneier; Chuck Bargeron, tech coordinator of BugwoodNet and ForestryImages.org; Zvezdana Ukropina-Crawford; Larry Allain, photographer extraordinaire; Diane Hoots of the KrazyKudzu website; Greg Krakow for the data at the Georgia Department of Natural Resources; Leslie Kimel for the introduction at the Georgia Wildlife Federation; Walter Reeves; Andy and Sally Wasowski; my dad Roger; my stepmom Joyce; and my husband Gene, who kept my fingers typing even when there was more on my plate than I could handle.

To my wonderful husband Gene, who sits and watches me pull out the laptop and automatically grins my way. In this grin, I find encouragement to put words on a page, page after page, until my ideas run their course. It is Gene who gives me the courage to believe in myself. He is indeed my rare exotic in the world of weeds.

INTRODUCTION
WHY CHOOSE NATIVES?

by Leslie Kimel

When planting your backyard wildlife habitat, not any plant will do. It is
important to avoid buying exotic plants, especially invasive exotics, and
instead choose locally native plants. Locally native plants are the back-
bone of any backyard habitat project. They generally require less chemical
input than exotic plants, which come from faraway places completely different from your backyard. The strange, new climatic conditions exotics
encounter in your yard—hot and humid summers, perhaps, or very cold
winters—can cause them stress. They whither and wilt, and as a result,
you find yourself constantly watering, fertilizing, and spraying pesticides.
Because they're comfortable and at home in your yard, locally native
plants don't require such pampering. Native plants are the easy, trouble-
free choice. Also, since they don't require chemical fertilizers or
pesticides, they're a healthy choice for you, your pets, and the planet.

Of course, not all exotics whither in American soil. In fact, some of
them like it so much that they become invasive, escaping from our gardens and choking out the native species in our woodlands and meadows.
Invasive exotics are a serious threat to biodiversity. Indeed, 42 percent of
the plants on the endangered species list got there because of competi-
tion from invasive exotics. Some often recommended invasive exotics that

should not be planted include Chinese privet, purple loosestrife, nandina, Cherokee roses, Japanese honeysuckle, elaeagnus, English ivy, and burning bush euonymus.

Plants like these threaten the survival of natural communities. In contrast, planting native flowers, shrubs, vines, and trees is the best way to restore natural habitats for native birds, insects, mammals, reptiles, amphibians, and fish. Plants occurring naturally provide native wildlife species with the food, cover, and nesting spots they need in order to thrive. Some exotic plants may provide songbirds with berries or squirrels with seeds, but what do they provide for flies, beetles, bugs, wasps, bees, spiders, and other tiny creatures that sustain and support food webs? At the bottom of the food web, native plants far outperform exotics. In fact, native plants support ten to fifty times as many species of native wildlife as exotic plants do. That's because native plants and wildlife have evolved together over thousands of years, and over time they have become dependent upon one another for survival.

Native plants make native wildlife species feel welcome and comfortable in your yard. They can affect people the same way. Native plants give your property something frequently lacking in new landscapes these days—a sense of place. Think about how frighteningly anonymous a new subdivision can seem. All the natural vegetation has been cleared away, and nothing but a few Bradford pears and an unnaturally bright, windswept expanse of turf grass surround you. You could be anywhere; you're nowhere. Planting locally native trees, shrubs, and vines helps restore this lost sense of place. Native plants bring back childhood memories; they are part of your natural heritage and personal history. Seeing them, smelling them, you know immediately where you are—you are home.

BOTANICAL EPITHETS

This book incorporates the Latin terminology of plants in an effort to avoid confusion over which plant is intended. I grew up calling forsythia "goldenrod" for as long as I can remember, and forsythia is definitely not the *solidago* "goldenrod." To help readers form a general understanding of a plant's characteristics based on its Latin botanical name, I have provided the following list of fifty Latin epithets and their meanings. I hope readers will use them as guidelines and perhaps feel inspired to pursue additional related information. I recommend browsing the books and websites included after the epithet list for more help.

Aborescens—tree like
Aestivalis, aestivale—of summer
Alatus, alata, alatum—winged
Albus, alba, album—white, pale
Angustifolius, angustifolia, angustifolium—narrow leaves
Aphyllus, aphylla, aphyllum—leafless
Aquaticus, aquatica, aquaticum—in water
Aristosus, aristosa, aristosum—bearded
Canadensis, canadense—Northeast American, Canadian
Clauses, clausa, clausum—closed
Coccineus, coccinea, coccineum—scarlet
Crinitus, crinita, crinitum—long haired

Diffusus, diffusa, diffusum—spreading

Dipterus, diptera, dipterum—two winged

Falcatus, falcata, falcatum—sickle shaped

Fistulosus, fistulosa, fistulosum—tubular

Flavus, flava, flavum—yellow

Floridus, florida, floridum—flowering

Fruticosus, fruticosa, fruticosum—shrubby

Geminatus, geminata, geminatum—paired, doubled

Glabra—hairless, smooth

Grandifolius, grandifolia, grandifolium—great leaves

Heterophyllus, heterophylla, heterophyllum—differently leaved

Humilis, humile—low growing

Incanus, incana, incanum—gray

Indicus, indica, indicum—Indian

Inodorus, inodora, inodorum—unscented

Laevigatus, laevigata, laevigatum—smooth

Laevis, laeve—smooth

Lyratus, lyrata, lyratum—lyre shaped

Maritumus, maritima, maritimum—of the sea

Maximus, maxima, maximum—largest

Minus, minor—smaller

Nivalis, nivale—of the snow

Officinalis, officinale—medicinal

Ovata, ovatum—egg shaped

Parvifolius, parvifolia, parvifolium—small leaved

Racemosus, racemosa, racemosum—with racemes, clusters

Rotundifolius, rotundifolia, rotundifolium—round leaved

Rubra, rubrum—red

Serrulatus, serrulata, serrulatum—small teeth

Stipulatus, stipulata, stipulatum—with stipules, blades

Strepens—making noise

Sylvaticus, sylvatica, sylvaticum—wild, in woods

Thyoides—citrus like

Tomentosus, tomentosa, tomentosum—hairy

Tripartitus, tripartita, tripartitum—three parts

Tuberosus, tuberosa, tuberosum—tuberous, a hump

Umbellatus, umbellata, umbellatum—in umbels

Viscosus, viscosa, viscosum—sticky

Other Useful Sources

Bostock, Peter, of Queensland Herbarium. Free DOS program that will translate Latin plant names to English. <www.ozemail.com.au/~pbostock>.

Charters, Michael L., and Calflora. Botanical Terms. <www.calflora.net/botanicalnames/botanicalterms.html>.

Glossary of Roots of Botanical Names from Garden Gate. <garden-gate.prairienet.org/botrts.htm>.

Griffin, Chuck. Dictionary of Botanical Epithets. <www.winternet.com/~chuckg/dictionary.html>.

Harris, James G., and Melinda Woolf Harris. *Plant Identification Terminology*. Spring Lake Publications, January 1, 2001. ISBN 0964022168. Neal, Bill. *Gardener's Latin*. Algonquin Books of Chapel Hill, March 1, 2003. ISBN 156512384.

Stearn, William. *Botanical Latin*. Timber Press, April 1, 2004. ISBN 0881926272.

GEORGIA ENDANGERED PLANTS

An Overview of the Sixteen Plants Endangered in Georgia

Baptisia arachnifera (Hairy Rattleweed, Hairy Wild Indigo, Hairy False Indigo)

Hairy rattleweed is found only in Georgia, specifically in Wayne and Brantley Counties. It is endangered due to clear-cutting, pests, and fungi affecting the reproduction of the plant. Leaves are simple and heart-shaped, unlike the typical trifoliate of the genus.

Echinacea laevigata (Smooth Purple Coneflower)

Smooth purple coneflower is found in only two counties, Stephens and Habersham. It is endangered due to collecting, highway construction, and power-line maintenance.

Isoetes melanospora (Black-spored Quillwort)

This plant is found in six Georgia counties, mainly in shallow water. It is endangered due to quarrying, cattle trampling, and littering.

Isoetes tegetiformans (Mat-forming Quillwort or Merlin's Grass)

Discovered in 1978, this plant is found in Columbia, Green, Putnam, and Hancock Counties. It is endangered due to quarrying, littering, and vehicle traffic.

Linderea melissifolia (Pondberry, Pond Spicebush, or Jove's Fruit)

This plant is found in Baker, Chatham, Screven, and Wheeler Counties. Pondberry is endangered due to timber harvesting and cattle grazing.

Oxypolis canbyi (Canby's Dropwort)

Canby's dropwort is found in Burke, Dooly, Lee, Jenkins, Screven, and Sumter Counties. It's endangered due to loss of wetlands.

Ptilimnium nodosum (Harperella)

This plant is found in Dooly, Greene, and Schley Counties. Harperella is endangered due to pollution and shoreline development.

Rhus michauxii (Michaux's Sumac, Dwarf Sumac, or False Poison Sumac)

This plant is found in Elbert, Columbia, Muscogee, Newton, and Cobb Counties. It's endangered due to low reproductive capabilities and habitat loss.

Sarracenia oreophila (Green Pitcher Plant or Flytrap)

This plant is found only in Towns County and is endangered due to land development and commercialized sales.

Schwalbea americana (American Chaffseed)

Chaffseed is found Baker and Dougherty Counties, extirpated from Baldwin, Early, Pike, Miller, and Worth Counties. It is endangered due to habitat conversion and forestry practices.

Silene polypetala (Fringed Campion)

This plant is found in Bibb, Crawford, Decatur, Taylor, Talbot, and Upson Counties. It is endangered due to logging practices and the spreading of the Japanese honeysuckle.

Thalictrum cooleyi (Cooley's Meadowrue or Savanna Meadowrue)

This plant is found only in Worth County and is endangered due to fire suppression and agricultural development.

Torreya taxifolia (Florida Torreya, Stinking Cedar, or Florida Nutmeg)

This tree is known only in one county, Decatur. It's an ancient genus, more than 160 million years old, and is endangered due to wasting disease first seen in the 1950s.

Trillium persistens (Persistent Trillium)

This plant is found in Habersham, Rabun, and Stevens Counties. It is endangered due to the limited range, clear-cutting, and collecting.

Trillium reliquum (Relict Trillium, Relict Toadshade, or Confederate Wakerobin)

This plant is found in hardwood forests in the Piedmont. It is endangered due to logging, mining, and the takeover of Japanese honeysuckle and kudzu.

Xyris tennesseensis (Tennessee Yellow-eyed Grass)

This plant is found in Bartow, Floyd, Gordon, and Whitfield Counties. The grass is endangered due to timber operations, erosion, and quarrying.

GEORGIA'S TOP TEN
EXOTIC PEST PLANTS

(List compiled by the GA-EPPC[1] and the Bugwood Network[2])

Pueraria montana (Kudzu)

Kudzu is a three-leaved deciduous vine growing to 35–100 feet. It is capable of extending more than 60 feet a season, at around 1 foot a day. Kudzu flowers from June to September.

Ligustrum sinense (Chinese Privet)

Chinese privet is a perennial tree/shrub that grows to 30 feet and flowers from April to June.

Lonicera japonica (Japanese Honeysuckle)

Japanese honeysuckle is a perennial vine that grows to 80 feet and flowers from April to August.

Hydrilla verticillata (Hydrilla)

The hydrilla is found in water and grows to 25 feet long. It flowers with tiny white blooms.

Sapium sebiferum (Chinese Tallow Tree)

Chinese tallow tree is a deciduous tree that grows to 60 feet, flowering from April to June.

Microstegium vimineum (Nepalese Browntop)

Nepalese browntop is an annual grass that grows from 1–3 feet and flowers from August to October.

Phyllostachys aurea (Golden Bamboo)

Golden bamboo is a perennial vine/shrub that grows from 16–40 feet and rarely flowers.

Elaeagnus umbrellata (Autumn Olive or Silverberry)

Autumn olive is a deciduous perennial shrub that grows 3–20 feet and flowers from February to June.

Wisteria sinensis (Chinese Wisteria)

Chinese wisteria is a deciduous perennial vine that grows to 70 feet and flowers from March to May.

Albizia julibrissin (Mimosa or Silktree)

Mimosa is a perennial tree/shrub that grows 10–50 feet and flowers from May to June. It was introduced in 1745 and now is seen rampant throughout the state.

GEORGIA NOXIOUS WEEDS

(List provided by Invaders Database System with profiles added by author[3])

Calystegia sepium (Hedge Bindweed)

Classified as a climber vine, the hedge bindweed is found in fields, in borders, and open woody areas. It grows at a fast rate and will choke out other plants if not watched carefully. It flowers from July to September.

Cardiospermum halicacabum (Love-in-a-puff or Balloonvine)

A delicate vine, this climber has tiny white flowers from late summer to early fall. The vine gets its common name from balloon-like fruit that contains stark black seeds. It is commonly found in various locations.

Convolvulus arvensis (Field Bindweed)

This vine flowers from April to October and is found in fields, pastures, and culti-vated land. Its seeds can live 30–50 years in ground before germinating, which makes wiping out an infestation of the plant difficult at best.

Crotalaria (Crotalaria or Rattlebox)

This annual grows quickly until it reaches its maximum height of 5 feet. It has green foliage offset by yellow flowers and fruits from summer until fall.

Cyperus esculentus (Yellow Nutsedge or Chufa Flatsedge)

This perennial grass has green foliage and flowers with yellow fruit. It grows rap-idly and can quickly take over an area. It blooms starting in mid-summer and produces fruit from summer until fall.

Cyperus rotundus (Purple Nutsedge or Nutgrass)

This grass is perennial with dark green foliage and purple spikes. It rarely produces fruit. Its extracts have been known to be a fever reducer and pain remedy. Its tuber extracts can be used as a muscle relaxer.

Ipomoea turbinata (Purple Moonflower or Lilacbell)

Ingestion of this flower causes hallucinations. It is an annual herb in the morning glory family. In China, its leaves are used to treat stomach ailments and its seeds are used in trauma cases.

Nassella trichotoma (Serrated Tussock)

This drought-tolerant perennial grass grows up to 18 inches tall. It is characterized by brownish green leaves that turn yellow in winter. Infestation began in 1988 when corrupted fescue seed arrived from Argentina.

Solanum viarum (Tropical Soda Apple or Tropical Nightshade)

This aggressive perennial is host to numerous pathogens like the tomato mosaic virus. Vegetable gardens perish quickly with soda apple nearby. It can produce an average of 200 fruits a year per plant. It has fine white flowers during bloom periods.

Xanthium (Cocklebur)

This annual grows 2–4 feet tall in a wide variety of locations. Its burs are football shaped and covered with prickly spines. The cocklebur's seeds are toxic to livestock, and the plant will decrease the wool value of sheep that graze near fields where it grows. In fact, it was a major concern in the cotton and soybean trade, causing up to a 75 percent loss in infested fields.

GEORGIA PROTECTED PLANTS

Several plant species are part of special watch projects in hopes of keeping them off the endangered species list. When at all possible, growth of the following protected plants in Georgia should not be disrupted. The items on the list below are arranged by scientific name. This information is current and correct as of January 4, 2004.[4]

Allium speculae (Flatrock Onion, Little River Canyon Onion)
Amphianthus pusillus (Little Amphianthus, Pool Sprite, Snorklewort)
Arabis georgiana (Georgia Rockcress)
Asplenium heteroresiliens (Marl Spleenwort, Morzenti Spleenwort, Wagner Spleenwort)
Balduina atropurpurea (Purple Honeycomb Head, Purple Balduina)
Baptisia arachnifera (Hairy Rattleweed, Hairy Wild Indigo, Hairy False Indigo)
Bumelia thornei (Swamp Buckthorn)
Cacalia diversifolia (Variable-leaved Indian Plantain)
Calamintha ashei (Ashe's Savory, Ashe's Calamint, Ohoopee Wild Basil)
Carex baltzellii (Baltzell Sedge)
Carex biltmoreana (Biltmore Sedge, Stiff Sedge)
Carex dasycarpa (Velvet Sedge, Sandy Woods Sedge)
Carex manhartii (Manhart Sedge, Blue Ridge Purple Sedge)

Carex misera (Wretched Sedge)
Carex purpurifera (Purple Sedge)
Ceratiola ericoides (Rosemary, Sandhill Rosemary)
Chamaecyparis thyoides (Atlantic White-cedar, Swamp-cedar)
Chrysopsis pinifolia (Sandhill Golden-aster, Pine-leaved Golden-aster)
Croomia pauciflora (Croomia)
Cuscuta harperi (Harper Dodder, Harper Love-vine, Harper Strangle-weed)
Cymophyllus fraseri (Fraser Sedge, Fraser's Cymophyllus)
Cypripedium acaule (Moccasin Flower, Pink Lady's Slipper)
Cypripedium calceolus (Golden Slipper, Yellow Lady's Slipper)
Draba aprica (Sun-loving Draba, Openground Draba, Granite
    Whitlow-grass)
Echinacea laevigata (Smooth Purple Coneflower)
Elliottia racemosa (Georgia Plume, Elliottia)
Epidendrum conopseum (Greenfly Orchid)
Evolvulus sericeus (Silky Morning Glory, Creeping Morning Glory)
Fimbristylis perpusilla (Harper Fimbristylis, Harper Fimbry)
Fothergilla gardenii (Dwarf Witch-alder)
Gentianopsis crinita (Fringed Gentian)
Hartwrightia floridana (Hartwrightia)
Helonias bullata (Swamp Pink)
Hexastylis shuttleworthii (Harper Wild Ginger, Bog Heartleaf,
    Callaway Ginger)
Hydrastis canadensis (Goldenseal)
Hymenocallis coronaria (Carolina Spiderlily, Shoal's Spiderlily,
    Cahaba Lily)
Illicium floridanum (Florida Anise)
Isoetes melanospora (Black-spored Quillwort)
Isoetes tegetiformans (Mat-forming Quillwort)
Isotria medeoloides (Small Whorled Pogonia, Lesser Five-leaves)
Jeffersonia diphylla (Twinleaf)
Leavenworthia exigua (Least Gladecress, Leavenworthia)
Lindera melissifolia (Pondberry, Pond Spicebush, Jove's Fruit)

Lindernia saxicola (Rock False Pimpernel)
Litsea aestivalis (Pond Spice)
Lysimachia fraseri (Fraser Loosestrife)
Lythrum curtissii (Curtiss Loosestrife)
Marshallia ramosa (Coosa Barbara Buttons, Mohr's Barbara Buttons)
Matelea alabamensis (Alabama Spiny-pod, Alabama Milkvine)
Matelea pubiflora (Trailing Milkvine, Trailing Spiny-pod)
Myriophyllum laxum (Lax Water-milfoil)
Nestronia umbellula (Indian Olive, Conjurer's Nut, Nestronia)
Neviusia alabamensis (Alabama Snow-wreath)
Oxypolis canbyi (Canby's Dropwort)
Panicum hirstii (Hirst Panic Grass)
Penstemon dissectus (Cutleaf Beardtongue)
Physostegia leptophylla (Narrowleaf Obedient Plant, False Dragonhead)
Pinguicula primuliflora (Clearwater Butterwort, Southern Butterwort)
Platanthera integrilabia (Monkeyface Orchid, White Fringeless Orchid)
Potentilla tridentata (Three-toothed Cinquefoil, Three-toothed Fivefingers, Shrubby Fivefingers)
Ptilimnium nodosum (Harperella, Piedmont Mock Bishopweed)
Quercus oglethorpensis (Oglethorpe Oak)
Rhododendron prunifolium (Plumleaf Azalea, Red Honeysuckle)
Rhus michauxii (Dwarf Sumac, False Poison Sumac, Michaux's Sumac)
Sabatia capitata (Cumberland Rose Gentian)
Sageretia minutiflora (Climbing Buckthorn)
Sagittaria secundifolia (Kral Water-plantain)
Salix floridana (Florida Willow)
Sanguisorba canadensis (Canadian Burnet)
Sarracenia flava (Flycatchers, Golden Trumpets, Yellow Flytrap)
Sarracenia leucophylla (White Trumpets, Whitetop Pitcherplant)
Sarracenia minor (Hooded Pitcherplant)
Sarracenia oreophila (Green Pitcherplant, Flytrap)
Sarracenia psittacina (Parrot Pitcherplant)
Sarracenia purpurea (Purple Pitcherplant, Indian Pitcher, Flytrap)

Sarracenia rubra (Sweet Pitcherplant, Red Pitcherplant)
Schisandra glabra (Bay Starvine, Climbing Magnolia, Wild Sarsaparilla)
Schwalbea americana (Chaffseed)
Scutellaria montana (Large-flowered Skullcap, Mountain Skullcap)
Scutellaria ocmulgee (Ocmulgee Skullcap)
Sedum nevii (Nevius Stonecrop)
Sedum pusillum (Puck's Orphine, Granite Stonecrop, Dwarf Stonecrop)
Senecio millefolium (Blue Ridge Golden Ragwort)
Shortia galacifolia (Oconee Bells, Oneflower Coltsfoot, Shortia)
Silene polypetala (Fringed Campion)
Silene regia (Royal Catchfly)
Spiranthes magnicamporum (Great Plains Ladies-tresses)
Spiraea virginiana (Virginia Spirea)
Stewartia malacondendron (Silky Camellia)
Stylisma pickeringii (Pickering Morning Glory, Pickering Dawnflower)
Thalictrum cooleyi (Cooley's Meadowrue, Savanna Meadowrue)
Thalictrum debile (Trailing Meadowrue)
Tillandsia recurvata (Ball-moss, Bunch-moss)
Torreya taxifolia (Florida Torreya, Stinking-cedar, Gopherwood)
Trientalis borealis (Starflower)
Trillium persistens (Persistent Trillium, Persistent Wake-robin)
Trillium reliquum (Relict Trillium, Relict Toadshade)
Veratrum woodii (Ozark Bunchflower, Wood's False Hellebore)
Viburnum bracteatum (Limerock Arrowwood)
Waldsteinia lobata (Piedmont Barren Strawberry)
Xerophyllum asphodeloides (Eastern Turkeybeard, Beargrass, Mountain Asphodel)
Xyris tennesseensis (Tennessee Yellow-eyed Grass)

GEORGIAS NATIVE FLOWERS

Georgia has more than 3,000 species of native flowers. Although the following is not a complete listing, it is a wide selection of plants with spectacular color, long bloom display times, and ease of growing within the region. Gardeners who wish to start a native garden should not have trouble getting any of the following plants to grow in their area. The list also mentions threatened flowers. Each listing includes the scientific name, the common name, and a brief overview of the flower.

Achillea   *Actaea alba*

Achillea (Yarrow)

Yarrow, depending on variation, will grow from 6 inches to 4 feet high. It's a full-sun, drought-resistant, fern-like plant. Blooming in June, if deadheaded[5] it will rebloom in September. Blooms range in the reds, pinks, yellows, or whites. Propogate in spring by division.

Actaea alba (White Baneberry)

A perennial herb with 2-foot stems, this plant has showy white flowers blooming in May. It produces ten to twenty berry-like fruits in July and August. Baneberry prefers partial shade. It is an old aborigine's medicine for rheumatism. Beware: All parts are toxic, causing skin blisters and gastrointestinal inflammation.

Actaea rubra (Red Baneberry)

This plant is identical to white baneberry, but the fruits are glossy cherry-red in July with twenty to twenty-four fruits. Red baneberry is slightly taller than the white version at times, growing from 2–3 feet. Expect delicate white flowers, although there are some variants. Beware: The fruits are poisonous.

Agastache (Hyssop)

This perfect addition to a bee/butterfly garden grows to 4 feet high. Its violet-blue flowers, which arrive in late summer, bloom until autumn. Keep this plant in well-drained soil. It is a colorful display, with color depending on the variant. Propagate hyssop by division in the spring.

Amianthium muscitoxicum   *Amsonia tabernaemontana*   *Anemonella thalictroides*

Amianthium muscitoxicum (Flypoison)

This perennial grows up to 3 feet from bulbs. Its blooms are white-greenish-purple, and it flowers in early to mid-summer. Flypoison is a spiky member of the liliaceae (lily) family. In 1788, Thomas Walter in *Flora Caroliniana* gave the plant its name. Beware: it is poisonous, especially the bulb.

Amsonia tabernaemontana (Bluestar)

Bluestar is a perennial that grows up to 3 feet. Its light blue star-like flowers come through mid- and late spring. It also has long leaves and produces pod-like fruits.

Anemone virginiana (Tall Thimbleweed)

Beautiful and unique, this plant has thimble-like green fruits. Growing up to 35 inches high, it is a member of the buttercup family. Five-petaled blooms are white and usually 1 inch in diameter. Expect them in late spring to mid-summer.

Anemonella thalictroides (Rue Anemone)

This lovely plant resembles a miniature Cherokee rose. A perennial herbaceous plant that grows to 9 inches tall, it is prized in woodland gardens. It blooms white from late winter to early spring. Native Americans made root teas from this plant that were believed to cure diarrhea and vomiting, although the plant is potentially toxic. (While there are no reports of toxicity for this variety, the genus has many toxic forms.)

Antennaria plantaginifolia   *Aquilegia canadensis*   *Arabis georgiana*

Antennaria parlinii (Smooth Pussy-toes)

This evergreen perennial is from the daisy family. It grows up to 9 inches tall and has several flower heads. Blooming late spring to early summer, it is pink or white. The foliage is bright green and distinctive, with non-felt leaves. Pussy-toes have been used as a diuretic, astringent, and antitussive. Plant in full sun.

Antennaria plantaginifolia (Woman's Tobacco)

This antennaria has the genera characteristic felt-like foliage and hairy fruits. It's a perennial, growing from 3–16 inches in height, and prefers dry soil. Blooms, which come from April to June, are white or pale pink.

Aquilegia canadensis (Red Columbine)

Despite its name, red columbine also has yellow blooms. This self-sowing plant grows from 2–3 feet and prefers full sun to partial shade. From May to June, it sports drooping blooms that hummingbirds love. The plant requires no special care, as it likes average soil and is adaptable to its surroundings.

Arabis georgiana (Georgia Rockcress)

This perennial requires full sun to partial shade. It produces white or yellow four-petaled flowers from March to April. Found in shaded limestone riverbanks, rockcress was first collected in 1841 by Samuel Boykin near the Chattahoochie River. Due to its rarity, please contact the Georgia Department of Natural Resources if you find rockcress on your property.

Arisaema triphyllum   *Asarum canadense*

Arisaema triphyllum (Jack in the Pulpit)

This plant grows next to watery slopes, waterfalls, or another water source. Growing up to 2 feet, it has purple-streaked green "pulpits." The plant's basal leaves remain in clumps at the base of the stalk. Its fruit is red shiny clustered berries. Beware: Its calcium oxalate crystals, which are present throughout the plant, are toxic to most pets. Use caution when choosing a planting location.

Aruncus dioicus (Bride's Feathers)

Bride's feathers produce beautiful creamy white blooms in late spring. With a height of 4–6 feet, these delicate airy blooms make a great backdrop for the property or as a border plant. Plant the flower in average moist soil and in partial shade for maximum growth.

Asarum canadense (Canadian Wild Ginger)

This is a great container plant and also serves well as ground cover. The brownish dark purple flowers grow under the foliage in early spring and have a light ginger aroma. The plant's rhizomes are edible just like real ginger. You can find Canadian wild ginger in wooded, partially shaded areas.

Asclepias purpurascens

Asclepias hirtella (Barrens Milkweed)

Found in sandy, rocky soil, this flower blooms from June to August on a single stem, producing pale green flowers tinged with purple. It grows up to 20 inches in height. The plant's seeds disperse by wind, so keep it enclosed for multiple growth seasons.

Asclepias purpurascens (Purple Milkweed)

This plant grows from 2–3 feet in pigtail pods and boasts pinkish purple blooms from May to June in sandy soils. Purple milkweed is perfect for butterfly gardens as monarch butterflies feed exclusively on milkweeds.

Asclepias tuberosa (Butterfly Milkweed)

This perennial herbaceous plant grows up to 2 feet. An original plant with hairy stems, it has milky juice and 1/2-inch diameter blooms. Expect orange flowers starting in early summer. This is the only milkweed with alternate leaves. Beware: The plant contains cardiac glycosides, which are toxic in large amounts.

Astilbe biternata (Appalachian False Goat's Beard)

This border plant reaches a height of 3–5 feet tall. It prefers partial shade and moist soil. The flowers are small and white with ten stamens, blooming on a branched spray. The plant produces large, bold foliage and does best with added nutrients from fertilizer. Divide it every four years for maximum growth.

Baptisia australis (Glade Blue Indigo)

This drought-tolerant variant grows up to 5 feet tall with a 3-foot spread. It thrives in full sun. The purple, spiky flowers, which resemble lupines, bloom from late spring to summer. Native American Indians used this flower as a purgative. Beware: The root of this plant is poisonous.

Baptisia australis

Bignonia capreolata

Boltonia asteroides

Bignonia capreolata (Crossvine)

This fast-growing plant is an evergreen vine that reaches up to 15 feet in length. It has tubular flowers—red on the outside and yellow on the inside when in the wild, and orange/red/purple when cultivated. It blooms from late April to May and prefers full sun.

Boltonia asteroides (White Doll's Daisy)

This plant has large white or pink flowers that resemble daisies and bloom from July to September. White doll's daisy grows from 2–4 feet tall and is adaptable. Helpful for naturalization and attracting butterflies, it should be planted in full sun or partial shade.

Buchnera americana (Bluehearts)

Flowering from June to September, this small, five-petal, dark blue bloom is usually found in prairies as a wildflower. It produces fruit from August to October and reaches a maximum height of 2 feet. It prefers full sun and well-drained soil. Water this plant moderately to keep it from drying out.

Callirhoe digitata (Finger Poppy-mallow)

This species has a traditional poppy look and is low maintenance. It grows to a height of 2–3 feet with a spread of 1–2 feet in full sun. Red and purple flowers with fringed petal edges bloom from May to September. Growing well from seed, this light and breezy flower is especially suitable for borders and meadows.

Camassia scilloides

Calystegia catesbiana (Silky Bindweed)

This endangered plant, a member of the morning glory family, is found sporadically in pinelands. Flowering from June to July, it blooms small and white on erect stems. The plant's trailing vine grows several feet, so use care to keep it corralled.

Camassia scilloides (Wild Hyacinth)

From April to May, this plant produces tiny, six-petal, star-like flowers from the lily family, usually in blues or lavender (rarely white). Wild hyacinth has a short bloom time, but the early bloom makes it an ideal addition to gardens. Its grass-like leaves grow from 1–3 feet high and spread from 1–2 feet. The plant prefers light shade and is found near streams.

Campanula aparinoides (Marsh Bellflower)

"Campana" in Latin means "little bell" and is the perfect name for this plant. The marsh bellflower grows up to 3 feet and has blue bell-like flowers on weak stems. You can propagate from seed. It blooms well from June to August in full sun and in wet habitats.

Cardamine laciniata

Campanula divaricata (Small Bonny Bellflower)

This bellflower, which grows from 1–3 feet, has clusters of bluish violet flowers that bloom in early fall. These light flowers prefer dry, woody areas and partial shade.

Campsis radicans (Trumpet Creeper)

Although this plant can be invasive, it flourishes on arbors or fences. Its trumpet-shaped flowers—in yellow, orange, or red—bloom on a woody vine that grows to 40 feet. Hummingbirds like the blooms. Full sun and rich, moist soil support this plant's rapid growth. You may propagate them from suckers and roots. Use caution, as the plant can irritate skin.

Cardamine laciniata (Cutleaf Toothwort)

Growing up to 8–12 inches, this plant sports lavender or pink four-petal flowers with three leaves per bloom. It grows best in full sun or partial shade and prefers moist soil. The root has a light peppery taste.

Chelone glabra

Cherophyllum procumbens

Caulophyllum thalictroides (Blue Cohosh)

This perennial grows up to 3 feet and has small yellow (turning to brown) flowers in clusters, blue-green foliage, and dark blue berries. Usually found in streams, it prefers shade and moist soil. Divide in spring or fall to propagate.

Chamaelirium luteum (Fairywand)

This perennial grows up to 4 feet with 6-inch leaves. Dense and spiky, the plant's white flowers fade to yellow. It prefers early sun and has evergreen foliage. The name comes from the Greek meaning "on the ground lily."

Chelone glabra (White Turtlehead)

This unusual flower grows well in containers. Reaching a height of 3 feet with a 20-inch spread, white turtlehead has serrated leaves and white, hooded flowers shaped like turtles. Blooms are white or sometimes pink or green. The plant prefers shade and moist soil, and you may divide in fall or spring. Chelone was a nymph in Greek mythology; she insulted the gods by not attending the wedding of Zeus and Hera and was turned into a turtle.

Cherophyllum procumbens (Spreading Chervil)

This member of the carrot family has small white five-petal flowers that last only a short time. The plant looks and smells similar to parsley. It prefers moist, woody areas and blooms from April to May.

Chrysogonum virginianum (Green and Gold)

This perennial makes a wonderful ground cover as it only grows 6–9 inches tall. It prefers full to partial shade and moist soil. Its five-petal blooms are daisy-like and appear in both spring and fall. It has dark green foliage.

Cimicifuga racemosa (Black Bugbane)

With tall spikes and white flowers, this perennial works well for borders. It is a member of the buttercup family and prefers deep shade. Black bugbane grows up to 8 feet and blooms from May to September. Its root was an official drug of the US Pharmacopoeia from 1820–1926. Today it is a popular alternative to estrogen therapy.

Cirsium carolinianum   *Cirsium muticum*

Cirsium carolinianum (Purple Thistle)

This biennial grows up to 6 feet and prefers woody areas. Its pinkish purple flowers bloom from May to June, attracting butterflies. It fruits from June to July.

Cirsium muticum (Swamp Thistle)

This plant, a member of the aster family, grows from 2–8 feet. It has webby foliage and large thistle flower heads. From July to September, it produces red and purple cluster blooms. It is a favorite of butterflies.

Clematis crispa   Clematis virginiana

Clematis crispa (Swamp Leather Flower)

This rapid-growing vine, which prefers partial to full shade, can reach 6–10 feet. Its bell-shaped flowers are blue, pink, lavender, or white. Its seed heads look like hedgehogs. Every year, swamp leather flower dies off.

Clematis ochroleuca (Curly-heads)

This plant prefers sandy grasslands. It grows 1 to 2 feet and prefers full to partial shade, making it a good choice for rock gardens. From May to June, curly-heads produce fuzzy cream or purple-red bells. The fruits are brownish white with curly hairs. Propagate from seed.

Clematis viorna (Vasevine)

From May to August, this perennial hairy vine produces urn-shaped red or purple flowers. It grows up to 6 feet and prefers shady, wooded areas. Vasevine fruits from August to November with dark brown feathery seeds.

Clematis virginiana (Devil's Darning Needles)

This deciduous vine is a rapid grower, reaching maturity at around 18 feet. It is a member of the buttercup family and can be found in thickets and streambanks. It grows best in full sun or partial shade. With distinctive string-like seeds, devil's darning needles produce white flowers from late summer to fall. The blooms have a faint fragrance.

Clintonia umbellulata (White Clintonia)

This perennial grows on 8–18-inch stems and is abundant with blooms. During bloom season from mid- to late spring, white clintonia usually produces five to thirty small white flowers with purple spots. It has shiny foliage and dark bluish black berries.

Coreopsis (Tickseed)

This fast grower from the daisy family grows on bushy 2-foot stems. It has a spread of around 1–3 feet. Expect single or double yellow flowers on long stems. Deadhead these for better flowering. Tickseed prefers full sun and well-drained soil. Propagate from seed.

Corydalis favula (Yellow Fumewort)

This herbaceous perennial can grow up to 15 inches tall. From late winter to spring, small, delicate yellow flowers bloom. Yellow fumewort grows in rocky and sandy soil. Beware: This plant may be toxic, depending upon the person and circumstance.

Cypripedium acaule (Pink Lady's Slipper)

Pink lady's slipper is the only cypripedium that requires an acidic soil. Test the soil before planting and make sure it has a range of pH 3.5–4.5. This flower blooms five to six years after first growth, with light to dark pink flowers from May to June. Reaching a height of 8–18 inches, the plant's leaves appear to grow right out of the ground instead of off the stem. Native Americans used pink lady's slipper to invoke spirit dreams.

Corydalis favula   *Cypripedium acaule*

Cypripedium parviflorum

Cypripedium reginae

Cypripedium parviflorum (Lesser Yellow Lady's Slipper)

A member of the orchid family, this plant grows 6–16 inches high and prefers well-drained soil. It is found in five Georgia counties—Murray, Towns, White, Habersham, and Spalding. From May to June, the plant produces predominately yellow blooms. Teas made from its root are known to alleviate pain and help in sleeping.

Cypripedium reginae (Showy Lady's Slipper)

One of the largest lady's slipper varieties, this plant sports multiple stems and grows 2–3 feet tall. In June or July, it produces white blooms with a dark pink slipper that reach up to 3 inches across, with one to three flowers per stem. Its foliage is lime-green with hairy leaves. Showy lady's slipper needs two to three hours of direct sunlight per day for optimum growth.

Dalea gattingeri (Purple-tassels)

This rare plant is found in only two northwest Georgia counties—Walker and Catoosa. Growing up to 6 inches high, the plant produces dense clusters of purple and sometimes white flowers on erect stems from July to September. Purple-tassels is drought tolerant and prefers sandy, loamy soil and no shade.

Daucus pusillus
(American Wild Carrot)

This herbaceous annual, in the same genus as Queen Anne's lace, has fern-like leaves and grows up to 2 feet tall. From April to June, it produces tiny white flowers. The umbrel[6] turns brown when mature.

Decumaria barbara (Woodvamp)

This pleasant-smelling ground cover is found all over Georgia. From June to July, it produces 4-inch white flowers in dome clusters. It only flowers if it has climbed as a vine. With semi-evergreen glossy leaves, woodvamp can grow from 25–30 feet in optimum conditions, including moist soil. The plant can last up to ten years in its native Georgia climate.

Delphinium tricorne (Dwarf Larkspur)

This herbaceous perennial is found in only four Georgia counties—Walker, Murray, Floyd, and Barlow. It can grow 2–3 feet high. From April to May, it produces violet or deep blue flowers (rarely white) that have five petals each. Dwarf larkspur prefers moist, rich soil. Beware: It is toxic to cattle.

Dicentra cucullaria
(Dutchman's Breeches)

This herbaceous perennial is found in six Georgia counties—Floyd, Walker, Murray, Union, Towns, and Rabun. Dutchman's breeches blooms in early spring, producing white four-petal flowers with a trace of yellow. Its outer petals form a "V." Many believed Dutchman 's breeches was a love charm, yet ironically it was also a Native American treatment for syphilis. Beware: The plant may be toxic, dependent upon the person and level of ingestion, and it can be a skin irritant.

Diodia teres   *Dodecatheon meadia*

Diodia teres (Poorjoe)

From July to October, this erect annual has star-shaped small white flowers on hairy stems. Flowers are four-petaled and can also be pink or pale purple. Poorjoe can reach up to 30 inches tall.

Diphylleia cymosa (American Umbrella Leaf)

This member of the barberry family can reach 3 feet in height. It is found in four northeast Georgia counties—Union, Towns, White, and Rabun. From mid-spring to late summer, the plant blooms with white six-petal flowers. It has leaves arranged on opposite sides of the stem and produces blue, berry-like fruit. The plant is slow to establish, so keep it in afternoon shade for better growth. Cherokee Indians used American umbrella leaf as a root tea to induce sweating. Beware: This plant can be toxic, dependent upon the person and the variety of the plant.

Dodecatheon meadia (Shooting Star)

From April to June, shooting star produces backward petals that are usually rose, lilac, or white. Its leaves are dark green and up to 6 inches long. The plant grows up to 20 inches tall on erect stems, but it usually takes up to three years to bloom for the first time after planting. Its fibrous roots are easily divided from the rosette. You will find this in seven Georgia counties—Walker, Catoosa, Whitfield, Murray, Gordon, Bartow, and Elbert.

Echinacea purpurea
(Eastern Purple Coneflower)

Characterized from June to October by a purple drooping bloom (rarely white) with a spiky brown center, this plant can grow up to 5 feet. "Chino" is Greek for hedgehog, and this plant is thought to resemble one. Eastern purple coneflower is showy, easy to grow, and a favorite for use in herbal teas. It prefers loose, sandy soil but adapts easily. Echinacea is the leading herbal remedy in today's market.

Echinacea simulata (Prairie Purple Coneflower)

A member of the aster family, this plant grows 2–3 feet tall and has a 1–2-foot spread. From June to July, it shoots single pink or purple flower heads on erect stems. For maximum results, plant this coneflower in full sun or partial shade. In herbal medicine, it is known to boost the immune system. It is also used as an antibacterial or antifungal.

Epigaea repens (Trailing Arbutus)

From early to mid-spring, this evergreen perennial produces three to five clusters of fragrant white/pink/red blooms (color depends on the variety of the plant). In late summer, berry-like fruits appear. Trailing arbutus is low creeping and serves well as a ground cover, but it is not drought tolerant. It prefers partial shade.

Epilobium angustifolium
(Fireweed)

This member of the evening primrose family grows up to 6 feet tall. It blooms from summer to fall with pink showy flowers on clusters. With seeds covered by white-brown cotton-like fuzz and deciduous green foliage, fireweed prefers full sun or partial shade.

Erigenia bulbosa (Harbinger-of-spring)

Found in two Georgia counties, Walker and Floyd, this early bloomer produces white flowers with reddish brown anthers from mid-winter to mid-spring. Appropriately, *erigenia* in Greek means "early born." Cherokee Indians chewed on this plant to ease a toothache. With its fern-like foliage, harbinger-of-spring works well planted with hostas. Rub a paintbrush over the entire plant to help it self-sow.

Erigeron pulchellus (Robin's Plantain)

This hairy-stemmed perennial grows up to 2 feet, blooming from mid-spring to summer with white flowers or lavender flowers that fade to white over time. Each daisy-like, thin-petaled flower has 50 to 100 rays. Found in more than twenty-five Georgia counties, Robin's plantain prefers full sun and well-drained soil. Medicinally, it was used as a tea for a diuretic and astringent. Beware: This plant can cause dermatitis.

Eryngium yuccifolium (Button Eryngo)

This plant grows up to 4 feet and has an 18-inch spread. For efficient growth, plant in full sun and provide moist soil. Button eryngo produces pale green to light blue blooms in mid-summer. A member of the carrot family, this ornamental plant is easy to grow. Divide the root ball to propagate.

Erigeron pulchellus

Eryngium yuccifolium

Erythronium albidum (White Fawnlily)

Growing up to 12 inches high with white or yellow flowers, white fawnlily has a bloom season of late winter to early spring. It prefers partial shade and moist soil. Rare in Georgia, it can be propagated somewhat by seeds. Expect to wait four or five years for the plant to flower.

Eupatorium coelestinum (Blue Mistflower)

This perennial grows up to 2 feet high and produces blue-violet flowers from summer to fall. Blue mistflower may be invasive in optimum conditions. It prefers sun to partial shade and can be divided by the root ball to propagate.

Eupatorium purpureum (Sweetscented Joe Pye Weed)

Sweetscented Joe-Pye-Weed grows 3–4 feet high with an equal spread. This carefree plant, which prefers sun or partial shade, produces pink, purple, or nearly white blooms from summer to fall. Bag the seed heads in order to capture the seed and propagate. Be sure to sow the seed as soon as possible, as it is not a good candidate for storage. Either cut to the ground in winter or leave unattended.

Eupatorium rugosum (Snakeroot)

A good choice to plant with solidago, this plant grows up to 4 feet high with a 4-foot spread. From August to October, it produces white flowers on erect stems. Butterflies are attracted to snakeroot. The plant's care is simple, and you can propagate it by dividing the rhizomes. Beware: Snakeroot is poisonous if ingested.

Filipendula rubra
(Queen of the Prairie)

This plant is a favorite of butterflies, birds, and bees. It grows up to 4 feet tall with a 2–3-foot spread. From spring to summer, it produces pink blooms. Plant in full sun and moist soil, and cut back the foliage when it starts to brown.

Fragaria virginiana (Virginia Strawberry)

From the rose family, this low-running perennial grows up to 12 inches high. It blooms from May to June, with five-petal white flowers and red fruit. Historically, the fruit of Virginia strawberry has been used as a gout remedy, and its leaves are a mild astringent.

Fragaria virginiana

Gaultheria procumbens   *Gelsemium sempervirens*

Galax aphylla (Beetleweed)

Growing 2–3 feet high on a 2–3-foot spread, this hardy ground cover is used to decorate wreaths. It prefers partial to full shade and moist soil. In mid-spring, beetleweed produces white flowers and bronzy evergreen foliage. Divide the root ball to propagate.

Gaultheria procumbens (Eastern Teaberry)

This small plant grows under 6 inches with a 15-inch spread. It prefers partial to full shade and acidic soil. In late spring, the plant produces white urn-shaped flowers, and in fall, red berries and aromatic evergreen foliage.

Gelsemium sempervirens (Evening Trumpet Flower)

A vine that grows up to 20 feet, evening trumpet flower can overrun a garden if not contained in pots. It produces bright yellow flowers in mid-spring. Many people enjoy its fragrance and appearance on mailboxes. Divide the root ball to propagate. Beware: Some parts of this plant are poisonous if ingested.

Geranium maculatum

Gentiana autumnalis (Pinebarren Gentian)

From August to October, blue or violet five-petal flowers, resembling lilies, adorn pinebarren gentian in groups of two or three. It grows up to 18 inches tall with thin leaves. Propagate it via seed in autumn, or divide in spring.

Geranium maculatum (Spotted Geranium)

From April to May, spotted geranium produces rose or lavender five-petal flowers. The seedpod resembles a crane's bill. The plant can reach up to 18 inches with shade and dry soil, preferring open woody areas. It grows well in rock gardens.

Goodyera pubescens (Downy Rattlesnake Plantain)

Despite its name, this plant is not a plantain. It can be a common yard weed. A member of the orchid family, this evergreen plant grows up to 18 inches tall. It produces white flowers from July to August, and its leaves resemble a snakeskin. According to legend, if you step on downy rattlesnake plantain in the woods, you will lose your way.

Helenium autumnale

Helenium autumnale (Common Sneezeweed)

This upright, hardy plant reaches a height of 4–6 feet with a spread of 3–4 feet. From August to October, it produces flowers in the red, yellow, and orange spectrum. Common sneezeweed prefers full sun and moist soil. Gather seed by collecting the seed heads when the flowers fade, or divide in spring or fall to propagate.

Helianthus verticillatus (Whorled Sunflower)

Anyone who finds this rare sunflower is asked to report its location to a conservation organization. Found mostly in Floyd County, it is a deciduous perennial and produces beautiful yellow thirteen-ray flowers from September to October.

Helianthus annuus (Sunflower)

This sunflower grows up to 15 feet high and flowers from spring to summer. The flower heads follow the sun, facing east in the morning and west at night—thus it is known as the "sunflower." It prefers full sun. More than 3,000 years ago, Native Americans cultivated it as a food source. Today, it is one of the most common seeds and used as seasoning and snacks.

Hibiscus coccineus   *Hydrolea ovata*

Heuchera americana (American Alum Root)

This plant has showy foliage with ruffled leaves. Preferring full sun or partial shade, it can reach up to 3 feet tall. American alum root produces reddish green flowers from June to July. The Cherokee Indians used the root as an astringent. Also, root tea was used to treat dysentery.

Hibiscus coccineus (Scarlet Rosemallow)

Throughout summer and fall, scarlet rosemallow produces five-petal scarlet blooms that reach up to 7 feet tall on erect stems. The blooms are 6–8 inches across and last only one day, though new ones continually bloom during the season. Before it blooms, the plant resembles marijuana. Divide the root to propagate. It dies out in winter, but expect it to resprout each spring.

Hydrolea ovata (Ovate False Fiddleleaf)

This perennial, a favorite of songbirds, grows up to 2 feet tall and produces dark blue five-petal blooms from summer to fall. Expect hairy fruits that attract wildlife. The plant prefers sun or partial shade. Ovate false fiddleleaf may be invasive, so monitor it and contain it if necessary. Deer resistant, the plant works well in bogs or water gardens.

Hymenocallis caroliniana
(Carolina Spiderlily)

This member of the amaryllis family grows up to 2 feet tall. From mid- to late summer, it produces three to nine fragrant white flowers. Carolina spiderlily prefers full sun or partial shade. Propagate this evergreen by dividing the tubers.

Hypericum prolificum (Shrubby St. Johns Wort)

This drought-tolerant plant with smooth deciduous leaves reaches up to 6 feet tall. A favorite of butterflies, bees, and birds, the plant produces bright yellow flowers in late spring to summer. It prefers sun to partial shade.

Iris cristata (Dwarf Crested Iris)

Growing up to 6 inches with a spread of 3–6 inches, this plant produces short-lived violet to white blooms from late spring to early summer. It is drought tolerant and prefers light shade and moist soil. Propagate by dividing the tubers.

Iris fulva (Copper Iris)

Copper iris reaches up to 4 feet high and has a spread of 9–12 inches. It likes full sun or partial shade. In mid-spring, it produces blooms that range in the rose/orange/gold/yellow/bronze color scheme. The plant works well in a water garden. Beware: Parts of copper iris are poisonous if ingested.

Iris versicolor

Iris versicolor (Harlequin Blueflag)

This plant reaches up to 2 feet in height and prefers full sun. From late spring to early summer, it produces blue-violet flowers. Harlequin blueflag has evergreen foliage and prefers moist soil.

Jamesianthus alabamensis (Alabama Warbonnet)

Ranging from 2–6 feet in height, Alabama warbonnet has bright yellow flowers in late summer and fall. It prefers full sun and has herbaceous foliage.

Liatris spicata

Lilium michauxii

Jeffersonia diphylla (Twinleaf)

This short-lived perennial ground cover grows to 1 foot high. It produces white flowers from late winter to early spring and prefers partial or full shade. Its dark, nearly black foliage resembles bloodroot.

Liatris spicata (Dense Blazing Star)

A favorite of birds and butterflies, dense blazing star grows up to 4 feet tall. It has violet to white flowers from mid-summer to fall and self-sows freely. The blooms resemble a feather duster. This low-mainte-nance, deer-resistant plant prefers full sun or partial shade.

Lilium canadense (Canada Lily)

This species grows up to 6 feet tall and pro-duces fragrant yellow trumpet-shaped flowers from June to September. It has lance-shaped deciduous foliage. Plant in sun or partial shade.

Lilium catesbaei (Pine Lily)

A good choice for a water garden, pine lily reaches up to 2 feet tall. It prefers sun or partial shade and moist soil. From late fall to winter, it produces red blooms. Divide to propagate.

Lilium michauxii (Carolina Lily)

Growing up to 2–3 feet tall with a spread of 2 feet, the Carolina lily produces red or orange petals that are bent backward. It can be found in the dry woods from July to August.

Lilium superbum (Turk's-cap Lily)

This perennial grows up to 10 feet tall and produces one to forty showy flowers from mid-summer to fall, with three to twenty leaves per whorl. Blooms can be orange, yellow, red, and white with a green star in the center. Cherokees made flour from the tubers.

Lobelia cardinalis (Cardinal Flower)

This perennial grows up to 5 feet tall and has toothed leaves. From late summer to fall, it produces red blooms. Its root was a Native American love potion. Beware: Cardinal flower contains poisonous alkaloids, so ingestion may result in death.

Lobelia siphilitica (Great Blue Lobelia)

This perennial herbaceous plant grows up to 40 inches tall with alternate 4-inch leaves. In mid-summer, it produces irregular-shaped blue flowers. The great blue's flowers are larger than those of most lobelias and have stripes on the tubes.

Lobelia siphilitica

Lysimachia ciliata

Lonicera sempervirens (Trumpet Honeysuckle)

This fragrant vine—a favorite of butterflies, bees, and birds—works well in wildlife gardens. Growing up to 15 feet in length, it prefers sun or partial shade. Trumpet honeysuckle produces red or yellow trumpet-like flowers from April to August. It has evergreen foliage. Propagate from stem cuttings. Beware: All parts of this plant are poisonous.

Lysimachia ciliata (Fringed Loosestrife)

This perennial grows up to 4 feet tall and loves partial or full shade. From July to August, it produces bright yellow star-shaped flowers. Fringed loosestrife has burgundy herbaceous foliage and ovate to lance-shaped leaves with fine hairs. Take care in containing the plant, since it can become invasive.

Maianthemum canadense (Canada Mayflower)

A perennial that works well in rock gardens, Canada mayflower grows up to 1 foot tall. It prefers partial to full shade and produces white flowers in mid-spring. Its foliage is shiny and textured. The plant is tolerant of acidic soil but thrives in rich, moist soil. Its red berries are a favorite of birds.

Marshallia mohrii (Coosa Barbara Buttons)

This threatened perennial grows up to 3 feet tall with a 15-inch spread. In mid- to late spring, its fragrant flowers are violet or white. The plant is an evergreen that prefers full sun.

Mertensia virginica   *Mikania scandens*   *Mitchella repens*

Matelea oblique (Climbing Milkvine)

This vine prefers light shade and has herbaceous foliage. Its flowers, which bloom from June to July, are greenish dark purple.

Mertensia virginica (Virginia Bluebells)

Virginia bluebells grows up to 2 feet tall, producing blue trumpet-like flowers from pink buds in April. It prefers moist humus-rich soil and partial shade. Divide in the spring to propagate.

Mikania scandens (Climbing Hempvine)

This vine grows up to 15 feet long. In late summer to mid-fall, it produces smoky pale pink or white flowers. It has herbaceous foliage and prefers full sun. Climbing hempvine can be invasive, so take care to contain it. Divide the root ball to propagate.

Mitchella repens (Partridgeberry)

This perennial only grows up to 6 inches tall and works well as a ground cover, with a spread of up to 18 inches. In late spring, it produces white blooms with bits of lavender. Partridgeberry has evergreen foliage and prefers partial to full shade and moist soil.

Monarda didyma (Scarlet Beebalm)

This perennial herb, with aromatic foliage and flowers, grows up to 4 feet tall. From late spring to mid-summer, it produces shaggy tubular flowers that are pink, red, violet, and white.

Myosotis scorpioides
(Forget Me Not)

This aquatic plant grows up to 18 inches tall and flourishes in ponds. It prefers light shade. In mid-summer, it produces long-lasting five-petal flowers that are medium blue.

Pachysandra procumbens (Allegheny-spurge)

This semi-evergreen ground cover, which prefers shade, is dense and solid. It reaches a height of 10 inches and is a slow grower. Allegheny-spurge has bluish green ovate toothed leaves. In April, it produces fragrant pinkish white flowers. It thrives in moist, well-drained soil.

Packera aureus
(Golden Ragwort)

This member of the aster family grows up to 3 feet tall and has yellow flowers. It spreads through stolons and prefers full sun or partial shade. Bloom season is May to June. Cherokee Indians made tea from golden ragworth and used it to treat heart conditions.

Packera paupercula (Meadow Golden Ragwort)

This herbaceous perennial from the aster family grows up to 20 inches tall. From June to August, it produces yellow blooms with approximately twenty flowers per head.

Panax quinquefolius (American Ginseng)

Usually known for its root's medicinal value, this herbaceous perennial can reach 20 inches in height. Its whorled leaves reach up to 10 inches. From mid-spring to mid-summer, it produces greenish white, five-part flowers. Native American tribes used the root to attract game or a husband.

Parnassia asarifolia (Kidneyleaf Grass)

With its alternate leaves and short height, this original plant is a quirky addition to any garden. It reaches only 8 inches and prefers a wet area. In late summer to fall, its blooms are white, five-petal flowers with green lines.

Passiflora incarnata (Purple Passionflower)

This hardy and fast-growing vine, with climbing tendrils, can reach 12 feet in length. Its flowers are 2–3 inches in diameter and are white with purple filaments. The white, fleshy center resembles a jellyfish. Purple passionflower prefers full to partial shade. Good soil drainage is a must. The plant blooms from July to September and dies back in winter.

Passiflora incarnata

Phacelia bipinnatifida (Fernleaf Phacelia)

This herbaceous perennial grows up to 2 feet tall on erect stems. It has alternate, lobed or divided leaves. From mid- to late spring, fernleaf phacelia produces small but numerous bright blue flowers with five petals. Before turning blue, the buds are white.

Phlox carolina (Thickleaf Phlox)

This fragrant perennial grows up to 4 feet high with a 2-foot spread. It prefers full sun. Blooms are typically pink, lavender, or white and are visible from June to August. Deadhead this plant to keep it blooming.

Phlox divaricata (Wild Blue Phlox)

Growing thick and low to the ground, this smaller variation works well when planted with tulips. It can reach up to 18 inches in height with a 15-inch spread. The blue/lavender/violet blooms last from mid-spring to early summer. Propagate from stem cuttings.

Phlox maculata (Wild Sweet William)

This perennial, with herbaceous foliage, grows up to 3 feet tall with a spread of 1 foot. From late spring to mid-summer, it produces pink/purple/white flowers. The plant works well for borders or naturalizing.

Phlox paniculata (Fall Phlox)

This phlox, a favorite off butterflies and birds, grows up to 4 feet tall with a 3-foot spread. It prefers full sun, moist soil, and good drainage. From mid-summer to fall, it produces fragrant, pinkish purple blooms. Divide it every four years for optimum growth. Expect a longer than average bloom time compared to other phlox.

Phlox stolonifera (Creeping Phlox)

This perennial—which makes a good ground cover when the fine, hair-like roots are not disturbed—only grows 6 inches tall with an 18-inch spread. Its blooms range from violet to lavender in mid-spring. An evergreen, creeping phlox is drought tolerant. Propagate by stem cuttings.

Phlox subulata (Moss Phlox)

This ground cover has needle-like evergreen foliage. With a moderate growth rate, it reaches up to 6 inches high with a 2-foot spread. It produces trumpet-shaped red/pink/violet/white blooms from April to May. Plant in full sun or partial shade, and propagate by clump division.

Physostegia virginiana (Obedient Plant)

This deer-resistant plant grows up to 2–4 feet. From late summer to fall, it produces lavender or pink flower spikes. The blooms open from bottom to top and work well in wildflower or water gardens. For best results, plant in shade with slightly acidic soil, and provide plenty of water.

Podophyllum peltatum (Mayapple)

A member of the barberry family, mayapple grows up to 18 inches tall. Its flowers, which grow under the umbrella-like foliage, are white with yellow stamens and have six to nine petals. Its berries look like lemons. Beware: All parts of mayapple, except its fruit, are toxic.

Polemonium reptans (Jacob's Ladder)

This plant spreads through creeping stems and grows up to 2 feet tall with an 18-inch spread. From April to June, it produces funnel-shaped lavender or blue flowers. It prefers full sun or partial shade and needs regular watering. Plant Jacob's ladder in an area with good drainage.

Polygonatum biflorum (Smooth Solomon's Seal)

This member of the lily family reaches 1–3 feet in height. From April to June, it produces small white bell flowers, and from August to October, it has bluish black berries. Its foliage has a fuzzy underside. Early colonists used the root tea for indigestion and coughing.

Polystichum acrostichoides (Christmas Fern)

This slow-spreading evergreen perennial grows up to 3 feet in height and spreads to an area of 1 foot. Drought tolerant, it prefers partial to full shade. Christmas fern fronds can be used for Christmas decorations.

Porteranthus trifoliatus (Bowman's Root)

This perennial has divided three-point leaves and beautiful fall color. In May, it produces a showy display of white or pink blooms. Bowman's root grows up to 2–4 feet in height. It prefers shade and average soil.

Potentilla tridentata (Shrubby Fivefingers)

A member of the rose family, this spreading carpet-like plant only grows to 4 inches in height. Its dark green evergreen foliage turns red in winter. From June to July, it produces white five-petal blooms. Optimum growth occurs in partial shade. Propagate by division.

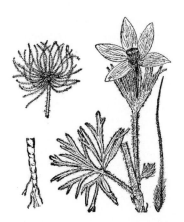

Pulsatilla patens
(American Pasqueflower)

This short, hairy perennial, a member of the buttercup family, only reaches about 6–8 inches in height. From March to April, it produces white, blue, or violet blooms. The plant, which thrives in rock gardens, prefers partial shade with moist soil.

Pycnanthemum virginianum
(Virginia Mountain Mints)

A favorite of butterflies, Virginia mountain mints works well in dried arrangements. It is a fragrant member of the mint family, producing white or pale lavender flowers from July to September. Growth usually reaches 2–3 feet in full sun. With its small leaves and low-maintenance care, this plant is a good choice for borders.

Ratibida columnifera
(Upright Prairie Coneflower)

Showy flowers on this plant grow up to 3 feet tall on erect stems. Lasting from early summer to fall, its blooms are daisy-like four- to eleven-ray yellow florets, 3 inches across. The plant prefers full sun. Great Plains Indians used this coneflower for tea and as a remedy for poison ivy and rattlesnake bites.

Rubus trivialis (Southern Dewberry)

This spiny vine has alternate leaves that are twice as long as they are broad. From March to April, it produces white to pink flowers. A self-fertile plant, its deciduous edible fruit is loved by wildlife.

Ruellia caroliniensis (Carolina Wild Petunia)

This is not a true petunia. From May to July, its blue or purple blooms reach up to 3 feet in height and have smooth leaves. The plant is drought tolerant and prefers partial shade. It works well as a border plant.

Salvia lyrata

Sanguinaria canadensis

Salvia lyrata (Lyreleaf Sage)

A member of the mint family, lyreleaf safe grows up to 15 inches in height with basal leaves up to 8 inches long. Its lavender flowers bloom in mid-spring and last through summer. The plant is drought tolerant and prefers full sun or partial shade. It is seldom planted but easy to grow. Native Americans used it as a tea for colds or asthma. It is also a folk remedy for cancer.

Sanguinaria canadensis (Bloodroot)

A member of the poppy family, bloodroot produces flowers that are white with yellow centers from late winter to early spring. The plant only reaches a height of 6–12 inches. It prefers partial to full shade. Juice from the root was used as a paint or dye in colonial times. Beware: This plant is toxic; do not ingest it.

Sarracenia

There are eight to eleven varieties of this plant. Sarracenia is so rare that the number of varieties is an estimate. Most of them prefer full sun, and all are endangered. This carnivorous plant grows as erect trumpet stems.

Sarracenia flava   *Sarracenia minor*   *Sarracenia rubra*

Sarracenia flava (Yellow Pitcherplant)

This variant grows up to 2 feet tall and produces bright yellow flowers from April to May. It has green, trumpet-shaped leaves with a hood well above the pitcher. The plant prefers full shade.

Sarracenia minor (Hooded Pitcherplant)

Growing up to 2 feet tall, this variant has white or translucent spots on the pitcher. The hood covers part of the pitcher, and yellow flowers bloom from early to mid-spring. Hooded pitcherplant prefers wet soil.

Sarracenia purpurea
(Purple Pitcherplant)

The leaves on this variant are bright yellow-green to dark purple. From mid- to late June, it produces pink to red flowers that are 2 inches in diameter. It reaches 1 to 1 1/2 feet tall. The plant prefers full sun to partial shade and acidic, wet soil.

Sarracenia rubra (Sweet Pitcherplant)

This sarracenia has red pitchers up to 14 inches tall, with a pointed hood and pale yellow flowers. It prefers full sun or partial shade and is perfect for bogs or water gardens.

Scutellaria elliptica (Hairy Skullcap)

Named for the hairy stems and leaves, this adaptable plant grows from 1–3 feet tall. Blue to lavender flowers bloom from May to August. Hairy skullcap loves sunny locations. Some Indian tribes used it to induce menstruation, introducing girls to womanhood.

Scutellaria montana
(Large-flowered Skullcap)

This endangered plant grows up to 22 inches tall. Less than 7,000 plants are recorded, with 90 percent found in Floyd County, Georgia, and Marion County, Tennessee. From May to June, large blue or white flowers bloom, and from June to July, the plant produces light brown fruits.

Scutellaria nervosa (Veiny Skullcap)

This endangered member of the mint family grows up to 2 feet tall. From May to July, small blue or white flowers bloom among simple, opposite leaves. It is found in wetlands or thickets.

Shortia galacifolia (Oconee Bells)

This rare white or pink flower has single funnel-shaped blooms from March to April. It grows up to 6 inches tall and can be found in moist, rich woody areas. The plant prefers partial to full shade.

Silene regia (Royal Catchfly)

A favorite of hummingbirds, this plant grows up to 2–3 feet tall and produces red blooms from July to August. It prefers full sun to partial shade and loamy soil. "Silene" comes from the mythical god Silenus, teacher to the wine god Dionysus.

Silene virginica (Fire Pink)

This perennial grows up to 26 inches tall. From mid- to late spring, it produces red blooms with notched petals. It prefers full sun to partial shade and needs moderate watering.

Silphium perfoliatum (Cup Plant)

This member of the aster family, a favorite of butterflies, grows up to 3–8 feet high. It has yellow rays from June to September and prefers full sun or partial shade. To propagate, divide or grow from seed.

Sisyrinchium angustifolium (Narrowleaf Blue-eyed Grass)

A member of the iris family, this plant produces blue, star-shaped flowers with yellow centers from May to July. It grows in grass-like clumps up to 20 inches tall and prefers full sun. Propagate from seed or divide every two to three years.

Smilacina racemosa
(Feathery False Lily of the Valley)

This plant grows up to 2–3 feet tall, and from April to May it produces a raceme of white flowers at the terminal end. A member of the iris family, it prefers moist soil and partial to full shade.

Solidago   *Spigelia marilandica*   *Spiranthes magnicamporum*

Solidago (Goldenrod)

This member of the aster family has fragrant yellow (sometimes white) flowers from mid-summer to mid-fall. Though it blooms at the same time as ragweed, it does not cause hay fever symptoms. Goldenrod grows up to 3 feet tall and prefers sun or partial shade.

Spigelia marilandica (Woodland Pinkroot)

A good choice for a hummingbird garden, woodland pinkroot has dark green foliage and grows up to 1–2 feet. In early summer, it produces bright red trumpets with yellow throats. It prefers partial shade and works well in borders.

Spiranthes magnicamporum (Great Plains Ladies-tresses)

This member of the orchid family grows up to 15 inches tall, and the leaves will fall off by the time the flowers appear in late summer. Blooming until fall, the flowers, which have a slight almond-like fragrance, are white with yellow and form in a tight spiral. Since this plant is somewhat rare, please report it to a conservation agency if you spot it in the wild or on your property.

Stellaria pubera (Star Chickweed)

This plant, which blooms from March to June, produces tiny white flowers with five petals that are split so they look like ten. Some birds like the seeds. Star chickweed grows up to 1 foot and prefers shade and moist soil. It was once used to fade freckles.

Stokesia laevis (Stokes Aster)

This plant grows up to 1–2 feet tall, and the leaves reach 6–8 inches. From early summer to fall, stokes aster produces long-lasting shaggy flower heads in the blue/lavender/pink/white color scheme. It prefers full sun and well-drained, light soil. Pinch off the dead flower heads for more flowering. This is the only species in the *stokesia* flower genus.

Stylophorum diphyllum (Celandine Poppy)

This plant grows up to 18 inches tall and likes partial to full shade. In early summer, its yellow blooms grow to 1 inch in diameter. Celandine poppy will self-sow well in good soil.

Symphyotrichum novae-angliae (New England Aster)

This plant grows up to 6 feet tall, spreads to 3 feet across, and is resistant to deer. Its pink or purple blooms appear from August to September. The flowers have forty rays and self-sow freely. Butterflies and birds are attracted to this aster. Propagate from stem cuttings, or divide in spring and fall every other year.

Symphyotrichum pratense (Barrens Silky Aster)

This critically imperiled plant produces lovely white, rose, or purple twenty-ray blooms in the fall. If you spot it, please report it to a conservation agency.

Symphyotrichum novae-angliae   *Symphyotrichum pratense*

Thermopsis villosa (Aaron's Rod)

This perennial grows up to 3–5 feet tall and spreads 2–3 feet. In spring and summer, it produces 1-inch yellow flower clusters. Aaron's rod prefers sunny locations and well-drained soil. The plant works well in borders or in flower-cutting gardens. Divide it or plant seed to propagate.

Tiarella cordifolia (Heartleaf Foamflower)

This plant, which works well as a ground cover, has heart-shaped leaves, a dense foliage mat, and reaches a height of 1 foot. In early summer, white flowers with yellow anthers bloom. Heartleaf foamflower is generally maintenance free. Native Americans made tea from the leaves and used it as a mouthwash for mouth sores.

Tradescantia virginiana
(Virginia Spiderwort)

This plant grows up to 2–3 feet tall. From early spring to summer, it produces blooms in the blue/pink/white/lavender color scheme. Virginia spiderwort is easy to grow and has grass-like foliage. Plant in partial shade and acidic soil, but don't add lime. The plant self-sows easily.

Tradescantia virginiana

Uvularia perfoliata (Perfoliate Bellwort)

This perennial, a member of the lily family, grows up to 18 inches high with a spread of 12 inches. From mid-spring to early summer, it produces single pale yellow (sometimes greenish) flowers with orange bumps on the petals. Plant in sun or partial shade.

Verbena canadensis
(Rose Mock Vervain)

This herbaceous perennial grows to 1 foot in height. In November, it produces pink/rose/purple blooms in five-petal clusters. Rose mock vervain works well in front borders. It is both heat and drought tolerant.

Verbena hastata (Swamp Verbena)

This perennial grows up to 4–6 feet tall and spreads to 2 feet. It blooms from late spring to mid-summer, with purple or white flowers on erect stems. Butterflies flock to this adaptable plant. The Druids used swamp verbena for purification, and the Romans made it into a torch for an altar. Early settlers believed it would ward off evil spirits.

Vernonia gigantea (Giant Ironweed)

This perennial, which resembles a blazing star, grows from 6–8 feet tall. Its flowers are in the pink/blue/red/purple range, and they bloom from July through September. Giant ironweed produces deer-resistant fuzzy foliage and self-sows. It prefers sun or partial shade. Beware: This plant is a skin irritant.

Veronicastrum virginicum (Culver's Root)

This perennial grows up to 3–6 feet tall with a spread of 2 feet. From July to August, it produces purple or white flowers that appear on spikes above whorled leaves. This unique prairie plant is drought tolerant.

Wisteria frutescens
(American Wisteria)

This fragrant, fast-growing plant gets up to 20 feet tall with a spread of 12 feet. Its blooms, which arrive in mid-spring, are blue or purple and resemble grape bunches. American wisteria is a woody vine from the bean family. Plant in sun or partial shade. Beware: The plant and seed are poisonous if ingested.

Zephyranthes atamasco (Atamasco Lily)

This plant grows up to 18 inches tall with a spread of 18 inches. It prefers sun or partial shade and moist soil. It has fragrant, nearly white repeat blooms that are single on fleshy stalks. It is classified as an amaryllis. Beware: Atamasco lily is poisonous if eaten.

GEORGIA NATIVE TREES

Trees significantly reduce the amount of air pollutants. If reducing pollutants is your main goal in adding trees to your garden, know that evergreen trees and shrubs are more effective than deciduous species. In Georgia, especially in metro-Atlanta, temperatures are up to 10 degrees higher due to tree loss. Loss of trees also increases the amount and severity of thunderstorms, reduces some levels of rainfall, and contributes to global warming trends. According to NASA, tree loss occurs at the rate of nearly 50 acres per day. However, in the last twenty years, Georgia citizens have replaced nearly 6.9 million acres of trees. The following is not a complete listing, but it provides many options from which to choose.

Acer rubrum (Red Maple)

This ornamental deciduous tree grows from 30–90 feet tall and up to 4 feet in diameter. Flowering from March to May, it also produces red leaves in spring and fall. Red maple prefers full sun but tolerates partial shade. It is widely used in the saw timber industry and as pulpwood. Whitetail deer consider the tree a food source. In the past, people made ink and various dyes from the bark. Use care when mowing and removing weeds around the red maple, as its thin bark makes it susceptible to damage.

Aesculus pavia (Red Buckeye)

This deciduous tree can also be a bushy shrub in some locations. It grows quickly to its mature height of 15–25 feet. From April to May, red buckeye produces dark red tubular flowers. Attractive to bees and hummingbirds, this short-lived tree (life span of only 3–10 years) prefers shady locations.

Amelanchier arborea

(Downy Serviceberry)

Serviceberry can be either a deciduous tree or a large shrub, growing up to 30 feet. It produces white flowers in March and reddish purple berry-like fruits from June to August. More than forty bird species eat the serviceberry's fruit, as does the gypsy moth. The tree works well in a butterfly garden.

Betula nigra

Betula nigra (River Birch)

Known for its paper-like bark, this deciduous tree grows up to 100 feet tall. It is resilient to flood damage and thrives in Georgia's clay soils. River birch requires a sunny location. Game birds love the tree's seeds.

Carpinus caroliniana (Musclewood)

Musclewood is a deciduous tree growing up to 30–40 feet high. It flowers from March to May and fruits from August to October. While it is forage for rabbits and squirrels, it is primarily considered a "weed tree."

Carya myristiciformis (Nutmeg Hickory)

This shade-intolerant tree grows well in Georgia's clay soils. It flowers from April to May and produces edible nuts from September to October. Hickory reaches a height of up to 65 feet. In the fall, its leaves are a brilliant yellow.

Cercis canadensis (Eastern Redbud)

This short-lived tree grows well in full sun or partial shade. It is also known as the "Judas tree," since it is rumored to be the tree from which Judas Iscariot hung himself. Redbud grows lives only ten to twenty years and reaches a height of around 15 feet. From March to May, it produces pink or purple (rarely white) flowers. Bark from Eastern redbud has been used as an astringent, and its flowers can be eaten in salads.

Cornus amomum (Silky Dogwood)

This tree grows from 6–15 feet. From August to September, it produces blue berry-like fruit that attracts birds. It flowers from May to June, with abundant but nonfragrant small white blooms. The silky dogwood favors partial shade.

Cornus florida (Dogwood)

This showy dogwood is one of the most popular ornamental trees in Georgia. It can grow up to 30 feet tall but typically stays around 15 feet. Blooming in spring, its heart-shaped four-petal white (or sometimes pink) flowers last two to three weeks. Birds like its red fruits. Though the tree normally prefers sun, Georgia's heat and humidity make planting in partial shade a better choice. Traditionally, people made tea from the bark and drank it to reduce fevers.

Diospyros virginiana (American Persimmon)

This slow-growing deciduous tree can grow up to 70 feet tall but usually stops at around 40 feet. Flowers appear from March to June, giving way to fruits from mid-September to November. Commercially, its wood is used for golf club heads and low-grade lumber. Unripe fruits have been used as a fever reducer, while ripened fruit is used to make ink.

Fagus americana (American Beech)

This impressive deciduous tree grows slowly but lives more than 100 years. Height for an American beech ranges from 80–100 feet. It flowers from March to April and fruits from September to October. In fall, its leaves are radiant yellow. The tree provides food for more than thirty species. Plant in a shady to partial shady area.

Fraxinus quadrangulata (Blue Ash)

The blue ash is a durable, drought-tolerant tree that grows up to 50–70 feet tall. In fall, the leaves are faint yellow, and it flowers from April to May. Commercially, its wood is used for flooring and crates. The tree's bark has been used to make blue dye. Plant in full sun for maximum growth.

Gordonia lasianthus (Loblolly Bay)

This tree grows up to 70 feet tall with a 10–15 foot spread. The trunk reaches 3 inches in diameter. In late spring, it produces fragrant, bright white flowers. Loblolly bay is an evergreen that prefers full sun, and it is often found growing with sweetbay.

Juniperus virginiana (Eastern Redcedar)

This magnificent, fast-growing evergreen tree reaches 30–40 feet in height and lives more than 450 years. The tree is named for its reddish brown bark. Birds are attracted to redcedar. It is shade intolerant and drought tolerant.

Liquidambar styraciflua (Sweet Gum)

Sweet gum, a long-living, shade-intolerant tree, grows between 50–150 feet tall. The tree can survive in most types of soil. Flowers bloom from March to May, and fruits appear from September to November. In the fall, its five-lobed, star-shaped leaves are red and yellow. Sweet gum wood is used for lumber and plywood. Traditionally, it is known as "copalm balsam" and is a medicinal substitute for storax. Other uses include chewing gum and a perfume agent for soaps.

Magnolia grandiflora

Magnolia virginiana

Magnolia grandiflora (Southern Magnolia)

One of the best-known trees in the South, the magnolia is a fast-growing ever-green that matures at around 60–90 feet. Its fragrant saucer-like white flowers bloom from April to June. Magnolias thrive in rich, moist soils and tolerate some shade. Instead of raking its leaves, let them fall around the tree and form a natural ground mulch.

Magnolia virginiana (Sweetbay Magnolia)

A slow-growing evergreen tree, this magnolia can grow up to 50–100 feet. It pro-duces spectacular white flowers from April to July and red fruits from July to October. The tree prefers partial shade. Two-thirds of all magnolia wood is used for furniture, but it is also used for popsicle sticks, tongue depressors, and broom handles. It is important forage for deer and cattle, making up 25 percent of their winter diet.

Myrica cerifera (Southern Wax Myrtle)

Also known as Southern bayberry, this evergreen tree can also grow as a shrub. It quickly reaches 40 feet tall. Flowers come early, beginning in February and lasting until June. It fruits from August to October. This tree is a source of wax for bay-berry candles, and it was cultivated in 1699 for use as a medicine source. The bayberry works well in a heavy soil landscape.

Nyssa sylvatica (Black Gum)

This deciduous tree grows from 60–80 feet tall. Its bark reaches more than I inch thick on older trees. Bees will use this tree for making honey. In the fall, its lustrous dark green leaves turn yellow, orange, red, or purple. Black gum prefers full sun for optimum growth.

Oxydendrum arboreum (Sourwood Tree)

Sourwood is a deciduous tree that grows 40–60 feet tall. It blooms late June to August and fruits directly afterward during September and October. It thrives in sun and partial shade. Leaves turn red in fall, and blooms are white in spring. The tree's wood is used for tool handles. White-tailed deer browse the sprouts.

Pinus elliottii (Slash Pine)

The slash pine can reach a height of up to 100 feet with a 3-foot spread. It has dark green needle foliage and looks lovely when surrounded by azaleas. Plant in full sun to partial shade and moist soil.

Populus deltoides (Eastern Cottonwood)

This rapid grower reaches up to 100 feet tall with a spread of 50–75 feet. It prefers sun and is drought tolerant. Eastern cottonwood produces cottony, non-showy flowers and modest fall color. Known for its easiness to transplant, it has brittle wood and simple medium-green leaves.

Prunus serotina (Black Cherry)

This deciduous, single-stem tree can grow up to 125 feet in height and 4 feet in diameter. It flowers in springtime and fruits in summer. Cherry wood is most valued in making cabinets and furniture. Historically, it was used in Appalachia as a cough tonic and a sedative. It can also flavor rum. Beware: Black cherry's leaves, twigs, bark, and seeds contain cyanogenic glycoside, which is toxic to livestock.

Populus deltoides

Quercus imbricaria

Quercus imbricaria (Shingle Oak)

Shingle oak is a deciduous shade tree that grows moderately fast to its mature height of 60 feet. It is adaptable in most environments but prefers full sun spots. This oak's wood is valuable timber, and its nuts attract birds. It has poor fall color but works well in a garden designed to attract wildlife.

Robinia hispida (Bristly Locust)

This small tree/large shrub has a spreading fan-shaped crown. It grows from 5–15 feet tall and is mostly ornamental. From May to June, it produces blooms in rose-colored clusters. It has grayish brown bark and prefers dry or moist soil.

Salix nigra (Black Willow)

This fast-growing tree reaches up to 40–50 feet tall with a spread of 30–40 feet. It has long, thin leaves and a leaning trunk. From May to June, tiny green flowers bloom. It is a short-lived tree, lasting only seventy to eighty-five years.

Sassafras albidum (Sassafras)

A sweet-smelling deciduous tree, sassafras grows up to 95 feet high. It flowers from March to May and fruits from June to September. Its wood is of limited commercial value, but the twigs make good forage for white-tailed deer. In winter, rabbits enjoy the bark. Native Americans used sassafras wood for making canoes. Uses for the tree's oil include perfumes and scented soap and antiseptic. Large amounts of the oil are a narcotic, but the tree's bark makes a good tea.

Taxodium distichum (Bald Cypress)

This slow-growing deciduous conifer can reach 100–120 feet in height when mature. Its lacey yellow-green foliage turns a brownish red in fall, and its bark is fibrous like a cedar's. Bald cypress prefers full sun or partial shade. Some species in Georgia have lived up to 1,200 years. Fruits appear in October. Budding in late December or early January, this cypress flowers around March and April. The tree's wood is resistant to decay and is suited for construction work, caskets, and boats. Its seeds are the perfect diet for waterfowl. Resins from the tree's cones have been used as an analgesic in folk remedies for skin disorders.

Tilia americana

Tilia americana
(American Basswood)

This deciduous tree has heart-shaped leaves and reaches 60–80 feet tall. It produces fragrant, pale yellow blooms in clusters of ten to twenty. It has gray or brown fibrous bark. The tree prefers full sun or partial shade.

Tsuga canadensis

Vaccinium arboreum

Tsuga canadensis (Canadian Hemlock)

This evergreen conifer grows 60–70 feet tall and lives more than 800 years. Hemlock prefers acidic soil and is shade tolerant. From 1880–1930, the bark was used as a tannin source. Birds are attracted to this tree for its seeds.

Ulmus serotina
(September Elm)

This fast-growing, shade-tolerant tree rises up to 80 feet when mature. It flowers in September (hence the name), and its light green fruits slowly turn brown when ripe. This tree is mainly used as an ornamental piece for landscapes.

Vaccinium arboreum (Farkleberry)

This small tree/large shrub, with trademark peeling bark, has evergreen leaves and tiny red buds. In mid-May, dainty white bell-shaped flowers bloom. Farkleberry produces black berries in the fall. It may reach 30 feet tall but is usually smaller.

GEORGIA NATIVE SHRUBS

As beneficial as trees are, shrubs are a close second on the list of most desirable to plant. Shrubbery adds 5–20% to your land value and provides texture, flow, and structure to your yard. With so many colors, sizes, shapes, and textures; you can surely not be bored with the selection. From a beautiful forsythia that sways with every breeze to the formidable *Rhododenron maximum*; shrubs are a fun way to put the whimsy back into your landscape.

Following are profiles of some of the notable shrubs in the Georgia area for your perusal.

Aesculus parviflora (Bottlebrush Buckeye)

This shrub grows from 6–12 feet high and prefers shady locations. Its four-petal white flowers smell like honey, and its fruits resemble nuts. In the past, Native Americans used the shrub's leaves as a treatment for colic and whooping cough. The wood is still used for packing crates. Beware: Leaves and seeds are toxic to people and livestock.

Agarista populifolia (Pipestem Leucothoe)

Also known as fetterbush, this evergreen shrub grows from 8–12 feet tall and produces bell-shaped cream flowers from May to June. Plant in shady areas for best color, and keep it watered because it is drought intolerant. Beware: This shrub's leaves, which contain andromedotoxin, are highly poisonous if ingested.

Amorpha nitens (Shining Indigo Bush)

This endangered shrub grows up to 9 feet tall. It has many blue flowers when in bloom, usually from May to June. The bush prefers moist soil and is found near creek borders and streams.

Aronia arbulifolia (Red Chokeberry)

This deciduous slow-growing shrub, a favorite of birds, prefers well-drained soil and partial shade. It can reach a height of 6–10 feet tall. In the fall, red chokeberry turns a brilliant red. From March to May, it produces white or pink flowers.

Callicarpa americana (Beautyberry)

This bushy shrub grows 3–12 feet and produces tubular flowers from June to July. From August to November, more than ten species of birds enjoy its fruit. White-tailed deer use it as forage. Beautyberry grows well in typical Georgia clay soils.

Calycanthus floridus (Sweetshrub)

This deciduous shrub grows 4–8 feet tall. Its shape depends on your planting technique; in full sun it grows tight and round, and in shade it grows into a looser, more open shape. Sweetshrub's leaves are fragrant when crushed, and from May to June it produces spice-scented rusty red flowers. The shrub needs moist soil. Its flowers and bark work well as potpourri.

Cephalanthus occidentalis (Buttonbush)

A deciduous shrub, the buttonbush grows up to 18 feet tall. From June to September, it produces tiny white blossoms, and it fruits from September to October. Bees use the shrub to help them make honey. In the past, people used its bark as a laxative and as a cure for skin ailments. Beware: Despite past uses, the bark of buttonbush contains cephalanthin poison that causes convulsions and paralysis.

Ceratiola ericoides (Sand Heath)

This evergreen shrub prefers dry, sandy areas. It grows up to 8 feet tall and produces red or yellow flowers in the fall. Sand heath has needle-like evergreen leaves and is drought tolerant. Plant in partial shade.

Chionanthus virginica (Grancey Grey-beard)

This deciduous shrub, which can also be pruned to grow into a small tree, is known for its light, wispy fringe—a result of the airy white flowers that bloom in May. Though slow in its growth, it can eventually reach 15–20 feet in height. Highly adaptable and an easy addition to any garden, the shrub should be planted in full sun or partial shade.

Clethra alnifolia

Clethra alnifolia (Summersweet)

This shade-tolerant deciduous shrub grows up to 8 feet tall. It has lovely reddish-brown bark. Summersweet is mostly ornamental due to the fragrant white flowers that bloom from July to August. It produces fruit from September to October but has little value to livestock and deer.

Crataegus triflora
(Three-flower Hawthorn)

Infrequently seen, this member of the rose family flowers from May to June with white five-petal blooms. It fruits from September to October. The plant is thorny, but consider adding one to your garden to help with its conservation. Three-flower hawthorn is often found on mountain slopes.

Dirca palustris (Leatherwood)

Like grancey grey-beard, leatherwood has light white fuzz, but it appears in winter instead of spring. Its winter beauty gives way to yellow flowers in February. This slow-growing shrub prefers shady locations. Even so, it is hardy and deer resistant.

Elliottia racemosa (Georgia Plume)

Used mostly as a shrub, the tree form of Georgia plume resembles the sourwood. It produces multi-flowered plumes that reach 15–30 feet high. Plant in full sun, as it does not tolerate shade. It flowers from June to July and produces fruit from July to August. In 1808, Stephen Elliot, its namesake, discovered it. It works well in sandy soils.

Erythrina herbacea

Erythrina herbacea (Red Cardinal)

This member of the bean family grows up to 6 feet tall. From April to June, it produces red showy flowers that hummingbirds love. It is drought tolerant and prefers broken shade. Beware: The shrub's bright red seeds are toxic.

Fothergilla major (Witch-alder)

A slow-growing, deciduous, suckering shrub, witch-alder reaches heights of 6–12 feet tall. In fall, its leaves turn red, orange, and yellow. In spring, it produces white spiky flowers, some of which have a honey-like aroma. Plant this trouble-free shrub in acidic but not limey soil and in full sun to partial shade.

Hamamelis virginiana (Witchhazel)

This deciduous, shade-tolerant shrub has numerous branches and grows 15–25 feet tall. Use caution around its thin bark, protecting it from weeds and lawn-mower blades. From September to October, witchhazel blooms, and it produces fruit but not flowers the next fall. The leaves, twigs, and bark have been used as salves. Twig extracts were once believed to give occult powers.

Hamamelis virginiana

Hydrangea quercifolia

Hydrangea quercifolia (Oakleaf Hydrangea)

This deciduous shrub grows 4–8 feet tall and is wider than it is high. During the course of its lifespan, its flowers bloom white, then pink, and finally tan. Bloom season is all summer, peaking in July. Oakleaf hydrangea has dark green coarse leaves that turn a variety of beautiful colors from October to November. Plant it in full to partial shade and mulch well.

Ilex glabra (Inkberry)

An evergreen shrub, inkberry grows 2–12 feet tall with dense foliage. Tiny white flowers appear from February to June, and red berry-like fruit arrive from September to November. Found in bogs and wetlands, this shrub would make a nice addition to a bog project along with *sarracenia*.

Ilex opaca (American Holly)

This evergreen shrub/small tree reaches maturity at up to 50 feet. Greenish white flowers bloom in April, and orange/red four-seeded fruits—favorites of more than eighteen species of game and songbirds—appear from September to December. The holly is shade tolerant, but heavy shade reduces its crown area by up to a third.

Ilex verticillata (Winterberry)

This yellow/green shrub grows between 10–15 feet high. From April to May, it produces tiny white flowers. Bulbous red fruits appear from fall to winter, remaining throughout the season—hence the name *winterberry*. Take care when weeding around the shrub as the thin, smooth bark is easily damaged.

Itea virginica (Virginia Sweetspire)

This slow-growing shrub reaches a mature height of nearly 8 feet. From May to June, its abundant white flowers are plume-like and arching. Virginia sweetspire works well in decorative gardens and is adaptable to most environments, from full sun to full shade. However, it prefers rich moist soil.

Kalmia latifolia (Mountain Laurel)

This evergreen shrub grows from 10–30 feet and is shade intolerant. It flowers from March to June. From September to October, its fruit are small round brown pods that release seeds. Medicinally, it was once used to treat bursitis, fibromyalgia, and arthritis. Its crooked branches make it an intriguing choice for your garden. Beware: Its wood is toxic to most livestock.

Lindera benzoin (Spicebush)

This shrub grows up to 8 feet tall and produces yellow-green flowers from March to May. When crushed, the shrub's leaves give off a spicy odor, making it a fragrant addition to your garden. From September to October, spicebush produces red fruits with a light peppery scent. Its leaves, twigs, and fruits have been used to make essential oils and fragrant teas. The dried powdered fruits can be used as a substitute for "allspice."

Osmanthus americanus (Devilwood)

This evergreen grows up to 50 feet tall but normally stops at 10–20 feet. It has a spread of 8–15 feet. Creamy white four-petal flowers, which have a sweet fragrance, bloom from March to April.

Prunus mexicana (Mexican Plum)

This large shrub/small tree can reach 20–30 feet in height. In spring, small wispy white flowers cover the shrub. A favorite of bees, birds, and butterflies, Mexican plum prefers full sun and moist soil for optimum display. It works well in a decorative garden.

Rhododendron canescens
(Piedmont Azalea)

This deciduous azalea grows 6–15 feet tall and produces showy pink flowers in early spring. It prefers acidic but not limey soils. The more sun it receives, the bushier the shrub will become. Divide the clumps to propagate.

Rhododendron prunifolium (Plumleaf Azalea)

This deciduous shrub can reach a height of 8–10 feet and be pruned into a small tree if desired. It is one of the last azaleas to bloom, with bright orange flowers arriving in summer. Plumleaf requires moist, acidic soil and partial shade. It is a good choice for attracting hummingbirds. It was first collected by R. M. Harper in 1913 (Fred Galle, *Azaleas*).

Rosa carolina
(Carolina Rose)

This deciduous shrub was named for the state in which it was first verified. It grows from 3–6 feet tall and produces pink flowers in May. Plant in full sun, and if you want to attract hummingbirds and butterflies, plant in groups. Rose hips (the fruit) are used for vitamin C since they are sixty times as concentrated as lemons. Rose hips are also used as a treatment for upset stomachs, for making jelly, and for teas.

Rubus occidentalis

Rubus occidentalis (Black Raspberry)

This shrub's berries, which many birds and mammals eat, turn red to black as they ripen. Its greenish white flowers arrive in May, and the berries ripen in June and July. Black raspberry grows on 4–6-foot canes.

Viburnum bracteatum (Limerock Arrowwood)

A favorite of birds, this shrub produces white billowy flowers from April to May. It grows up to 10 feet high. It has the dark green leaves and bluish purple fruits characteristic of arrowwoods. Alvan Chapman in Floyd County, Georgia, first discovered it. Limerock is a hardy shrub, though it prefers full sun to partial shade.

Viburnum rafinesquianum (Limerock Downy Arrowwood)

Another favorite of birds, this arrowwood grows up to 10 feet and is erect or spreading. It is drought tolerant and prefers sun to partial shade. Creamy white lace-like flowers bloom from May to June, and black fruits appear from August to September.

Xanthorhiza simplicissima (Yellowroot)

This woody shrub, which grows up to 3 feet high, turns a brilliant purple in the fall. Its flowers, which bloom in mid- to late spring, are star-shaped. Plant in partial to full shade for optimum growth. Traditionally, Native Americans used the roots to make yellow dye and to make teas that treated mouth ulcers, colds, or jaundice. Propagate yellowroot by its underground runners.

GEORGIA NATIVE GRASSES

Ornamental grasses add fluid motion to all seasons. Some are designed for summer show, others for winter color. They may be called grasses, but they are anything but mere green. Gold, maroon, pink, even silver or blue can be found. They wave and shine and can even sigh on a windy day. If shrubs add whimsy; grasses add a touch of romance to your landscape. They look frail and susceptible but ironically are hardy to the elements, pests, and diseases. They attract birds and wildlife with their seeds and their coverage. The biggest joy? No mowing!

Following are some grasses found in most parts of Georgia and will be designed for our zone climate. Try to resist planting just the pampas grass you see in the nursery; be brave and experiment!

Acorus gramineus (Striped Sweet Flag)

This grass is a semi-evergreen aquatic perennial that grows up to 6–14 inches. It prefers full sun to partial shade and produces barely noticeable horn-shaped flowers in mid-spring. Striped sweet flag works well in ponds. Propagate easily by dividing rhizomes in the spring.

Carex purpurifera (Purple Sedge)

Easily identified by its dark purple stems and bluish green leaves, this tufted perennial blooms from April to May and fruits from May to July. Purple sedge is on the threatened natives list and is only found in five Georgia counties—Walker, Chatooga, Floyd, Union, and Rabun. Search for it in rich woodland soil, and please report it to a conservation agency if you spot it.

Chasmanthium latifolium (Northern Sea Oats, Riveroats)

This drought- and salt-tolerant grass grows up to 3 feet high. It has 8-inch leaves and turns from green to brown throughout the seasons. The grass needs partial shade for prime growth. Expect its flowering in June.

Muhlenbergia capillaries (Pink Muhly)

A semi-evergreen that prefers full sun or partial shade, this grass has bright summer color. Use its as an ornamental grass for borders or backgrounds. In late summer to early fall, it produces pink blooms that are mist-like flowerheads. It grows up to 5 feet high.

Muhlenbergia sylvatica (Woodland Muhly)

This hairy-stemmed perennial grows up to 3 feet tall. It flowers from July to October. Commonly found along streambanks and in rocky, wooded areas, woodland muhly adds texture to gardens.

Panicum virgatum (Switchgrass)

A slow-spreading perennial with textured blades, red-tinged switchgrass grows 3–6 feet high. While adaptable to its location, it prefers full sun. It produces airy flowers from August to September, and its seed heads look like pillowy clouds. Switchgrass works well in wildflower meadows.

Schizachyrium scorparium   *Sorghastrum nutans*   *Spartina pectinata*

Schizachyrium scorparium (Bluestem)

This clump-forming, dark green, drought-tolerant grass reaches 20–40 inches high in fertile soil. It prefers full sun or partial shade and has a lavender/blue tinge on the base of its stems. In fall, look for a brilliant bronze color.

Sorghastrum nutans (Indian Grass)

Upright and fountain-like, this showy grass works well in borders or as an ornamental touch. It seeds from July to August, turning from green to tan in winter. Plant in full sun for optimal bloom of seed heads and plume.

Spartina pectinata (Prairie Grass)

This drought-tolerant grass works well in dried arrangements. It grows up to 6 feet and flowers June to October. Its hairy scales cause hay fever symptoms in some people. The color ranges from bright, clear yellow in the fall to buff in the winter.

Sporobolus heterolepis (Prairie Dropseed)

This slow-growing grass reaches 18–30 inches tall. Its upright leaves are green in summer and gold in fall. Prairie dropseed prefers full sun to partial shade and likes dry, rocky locations. It produces pinkish fragrant flowers from June until frost, and birds love its nutritious seeds. This grass is drought and heat tolerant.

RARE FLORA:
A COUNTY-BY-COUNTY LISTING 7

Please keep in mind the limitations of the database. The data collected by
the Georgia Natural Heritage Program comes from a variety of sources,
including museum and herbarium records, literature, and reports from
individuals and organizations, as well as field surveys by our staff biolo-
gists. In most cases the information is not the result of a recent on-site
survey by our staff. Many areas of Georgia have never been surveyed thoroughly. Therefore, the Georgia Natural Heritage Program can only
occasionally provide definitive information on the presence or absence of
rare species on a given site. Our files are updated constantly as new information is received. Thus, information provided by our program represents
the existing data in our files at the time of the request and should not be
considered a final statement on the species or area under consideration.

* *Georgia protected* | † *Federal protected*

APPLING

Callirhoe triangulata Clustered Poppy-mallow

Carex dasycarpa Velvet Sedge*

Evolvulus sericeus var. sericeus Creeping Morning Glory*

Iris tridentata Savanna Iris

Liatris pauciflora Few-flower Gayfeather

Marshallia ramosa Pineland Barbara Buttons*

Penstemon dissectus Grit Beardtongue*

Phaseolus polystachios var. sinuatus Trailing Bean-vine

Quercus austrina Bluff White Oak

Rhynchospora crinipes Bearded Beaksedge

Sarracenia flava Yellow Flytrap*

Sarracenia minor Hooded Pitcherplant*

Sideroxylon sp. I[8] Ohoopee Bumelia

Spermacoce glabra Smooth Buttonweed

ATKINSON

Palafoxia integrifolia Palafoxia

Sarracenia flava Yellow Flytrap*

Sarracenia minor Hooded Pitcherplant*

BACON

Sarracenia flava Yellow Flytrap*

Sarracenia minor Hooded Pitcherplant*

Tradescantia roseolens Rosy Spiderwort

BAKER

Arnoglossum diversifolium Variable-leaf Indian-plantain*

Asplenium heteroresiliens Wagner Spleenwort*

Carex dasycarpa Velvet Sedge*

Carex decompositia Cypress-knee Sedge

Carex fissa var. aristata Sedge

Crataegus brachyacantha Blueberry Hawthorn

Croton elliottii Elliott Croton

Echinodorus parvulus Dwarf Burhead

Epidendrum conopseum Green-fly Orchid*

Evolvulus sericeus var. sericeus Creeping Morning Glory*

Fimbristylis perpusilla Harper Fimbry*

Hygrophilia lacustris Hygrophilia

Leitneria floridana Corkwood

Lindera melissifolia Pondberry†

Litsea aestivalis Pondspice*

Lobelia boykinii Boykin Lobelia

Ludwigia spathulata Creeping Smallflower Seedbox

Oldenlandia boscii Bluets

Panicum neuranthum Panic Grass

Physostegia angustifolia Narrowleaf Obedient Plant

Polygala balduinii White Milkwort

Polygala leptostachys Georgia Milkwort

Pteroglossaspis ecristata Wild Coco

Rhexia aristosa Awned Meadowbeauty

Rhynchospora thornei Thorne's Beakrush

Schwalbea americana Chaffseed†

Scirpus hallii Hall Bulrush

Sida elliottii Elliott's Fanpetals

Sideroxylon thornei Swamp Buckthorn*

Spiranthes longilabris Giant Spiral Ladies-tresses

Thelypteris ovata Ovate Maiden Fern

BALDWIN

No endangered plants in Baldwin County, Georgia.

BANKS

Melanthium woodii Ozark Bunchflower*

BARROW

Cypripedium acaule Pink Lady's Slipper*

Pilularia americana American Pillwort

BARTOW

Acorus americanus Sweetflag

Alnus maritime Seaside Alder

Aster novae-angliae New England Aster

Berberis canadensis American Barberry

Buchnera americana Bluehearts

Calystegia catesbeiana ssp. sericata Silky Bindweed

Camassia scilloides Wild Hyacinth

Carex buxbaumii Brown Bog Sedge

Cheilanthes alabamensis Alabama Lipfern

Crataegus triflora Three-flower Hawthorn

Delphinium tricorne Dwarf Larkspur

Dryopteris celsa Log Fern

Fothergilla major Mountain Witch-alder

Glyceria pallida Pale Manna-grass

Hottonia inflate Featherfoil

Oldenlandia boscii Bluets

Panax quinquefolius American Ginseng

Phacelia fimbriata Fringed Phacelia

Rudbeckia heliopsidis Little River Black-eyed Susan

Schisandra glabra Bay Starvine*

Trillium lancifolium Lanceleaf Trillium

Viburnum rafinesquianum var. rafinesquianum Downy Arrowwood

Xyris tennesseensis Tennessee Yellow-eyed Grass†

BEN HILL

Balduina atropurpurea Purple Honeycomb Head*

Elliottia racemosa Georgia Plume*

Lechea deckertii Deckert Pinweed

Litsea aestivalis Pondspice*

Macranthera flammea Flame Flower

Marshallia ramosa Pineland Barbara Buttons*

Penstemon dissectus Grit Beardtongue*

Sarracenia flava Yellow Flytrap*

Sarracenia minor Hooded Pitcherplant*

Scutellaria ocmulgee Ocmulgee Skullcap*

Spermacoce glabra Smooth Buttonweed

Tillandsia setacea Pine-needle Air-plant

Vitis palmate Catbird Grape

BERRIEN

Angelica dentata Sandhill Angelica

Lobelia boykinii Boykin Lobelia

Macbridea caroliniana Carolina Bogmint

Myriophyllum laxum Lax Water-milfoil*

Pteroglossaspis ecristata Wild Coco

Sarracenia flava Yellow Flytrap*

Sarracenia minor Hooded Pitcherplant*

Sarracenia psittacina Parrot Pitcherplant*

Sporobolus teretifolius Wire-leaf Dropseed

BIBB

Sarracenia flava Yellow Flytrap*

Sarracenia rubra Sweet Pitcherplant†

Scutellaria ocmulgee Ocmulgee Skullcap*

Silene ovata Mountain Catchfly

Silene polypetala Fringed Campion†

Trillium reliquum Relict Trillium†

BLECKLEY

Astragalus michauxii Sandhill Milkvetch

Scutellaria ocmulgee Ocmulgee Skullcap*

Silene ovata Mountain Catchfly

Trillium reliquum Relict Trillium†

BRANTLEY

Baldunia atropurpurea Purple Honeycomb Head*

Baptisia arachnifera Hairy Rattleweed†

Cternium floridanum Florida Orange-grass

Fothergilla gardenii Dwarf Witch-alder*

Galactia floridana Florida Milk-pea

Ilex amelanchier Serviceberry Holly

Myrica inodora Odorless Bayberry

Palafoxia integrifolia Palafoxia

Plantago sparsiflora Pineland Plantain

Pteroglossaspis ecristata Wild Coco

Quercus chapmanii Chapman Oak

Rhexia nuttallii Nuttall Meadowbeauty

Sarracenia minor Hooded Pitcherplant*

Tillandsia bartramii Bartram's Air-plant

Xyris drummondii Drummond Yellow-eyed Grass

BROOKS

Agalinis divaricata Pineland Purple Foxglove

Baptisia lecontei Leconte Wild Indigo

Drosera tracyi Tracy's Dew-threads

Epidendrum conopseum Green-fly Orchid*

Polygonum meisnerianum var. beyrichianum Meisner's Tear-thumb

Quercus austrina Bluff White Oak

Sarracenia flava Yellow Flytrap*

Sarracenia minor Hooded Pitcherplant*

BRYAN

Amorpha georgiana var. georgiana Georgia Indigo-bush

Elliottia racemosa Georgia Plume*

Epidendrum conopseum Green-fly Orchid*

Illicium parviflorum Yellow Anise-tree

Liatris pauciflora Few-flower Gay-feather

Litsea aestivalis Pondspice*

Malaxis spicata Florida Adders-mouth

Mikania cordifolia Heartleaf Climbing Hempweed

Physostegia leptophylla Tidal Marsh Obedient Plant*

Platathera nivea Snowy Orchid

Ponthieva racemosa Shadow-witch Orchid

Rhynchospora torreyana Torrey Beakrush

Sarracenia minor Hooded Pitcherplant*

Stewartia malacodendron Silky Camellia*

Zenobia pulverulenta Zenobia

BULLOCK

Agalinis aphylla Scale-leaf Purple Foxglove

Amorpha georgiana var. georgiana Georgia Indigo-bush

Andropogon mohrii Bog Bluestem

Astragalus michauxii Sandhill Milkvetch

Baldiuna atropurpurea Purple Honeycomb Head*

Elliottia racemosa Georgia Plume*

Epidendrum conopseum Green-fly Orchid*

Hypericum sp.3 Georgia St. Johnswort

Ilex amelanchier Serviceberry Holly

Lobelia boykinii Boykin Lobelia

Oxypolis ternata Savanna Cowbane

Sarracenia flava Yellow Flytrap*

Sarracenia minor Hooded Pitcherplant*

Sarracenia psittacina Parrot Pitcherplant*

Sarracenia rubra Sweet Pitcherplant†

Scutellaria mellichampii Skullcap

Sporobolus teretifolius Wire-leaf Dropseed

Stewartia malacodendron Silky Camellia*

Stokesia laevis Stokes Aster

BURKE

Ceratiola ericoides Rosemary
Dryopteris celsa Log Fern
Elliottia racemosa Georgia Plume*
Lindera subcoriacea Bog Spicebush
Nestronia umbellula Indian Olive*
Oxypolis canbyi Canby Dropwort†
Quercus austrina Bluff White Oak
Sarracenia minor Hooded Pitcherplant*
Sarracenia rubra Sweet Pitcherplant†
Scutellaria ocmulgee Ocmulgee
   Skullcap*
Silene caroliniana Carolina Pink
Stewartia malacodendron Silky
   Camellia*

BUTTS

Amphianthus pusillus Pool Sprite†
Isoetes melanospora Black-spored
   Quillwort†
Pilularia americana American Pillwort

CALHOUN

Aristida simpliciflora Chapman
   Three-awn grass
Coreopsis integrifolia Tickseed
Elyonurus tripsacoides Pan-american
   Balsamscale
Lindera melissifolia Pondberry†
Lobelia boykinii Boykin Lobelia
Lythrum curtissii Curtiss Loosestrife*
Panicum hirstii Hirst Panic Grass†
Physostegia angustifolia Narrowleaf
   Obedient Plant
Plantago sparsiflora Pineland Plantain
Rhexia aristosa Awned Meadowbeauty
Rhynchospora decurrens Swamp-forest
   Beaksedge
Rhynchospora thornei Thorne's
   Beakrush
Sarracenia flava Yellow Flytrap*

Sarracenia minor Hooded Pitcherplant*
Selaginella ludoviciana Lousiana
   Spikemoss
Sideroxylon thornei Swamp Buckthorn*
Stewartia malacodendron Silky
   Camellia*
Xyris scabrifolia Harper Yellow-eyed
   Grass

CAMDEN

Acacia farnesiana Sweet
   Acacia
Asimina pygmaea Dwarf Pawpaw
Asplenium heteroresiliens Wagner
   Spleenwort*
Calopogon multiflorus Many-flowered
   Grass-pink
Carex dasycarpa Velvet Sedge*
Ctenium floridanum Florida Orange-grass
Eleocharis albida White Spikerush
Eleocharis montevidensis Spikerush
Elyonurus tripsacoides Pan-american
   Balsamscale
Epidendrum conopseum Green-fly
   Orchid*
Forestiera godfreyi Godfrey Privet
Forestiera segregata Florida Privet
Fuirena longa Umbrella Sedge
Justicia angusta Narrowleaf Water-willow
Litsea aestivalis Pondspice*
Lycium carolinianum Carolina Wolfberry
Phlebodium aureum Goldfoot Fern
Plantago sparsiflora Pineland Plantain
Polygonum glaucum Sea-beach
   Knotweed
Pteroglossaspis ecristata Wild Coco
Quercus austrina Bluff White Oak
Quercus chapmanii Chapman Oak
Sageretia minutiflora Tiny-leaf
   Buckthorn*
Sapindus saponaria Soapberry
Sarracenia minor Hooded Pitcherplant*

Thalia dealbata Flag

Tillandsia bartramii Bartram's Air-plant

Tillandsia fasciculata Quill-leaf Air-plant

Tillandsia recurvata Ball-moss*

Vitis palmata Catbird Grape

Vittaria lineata Shoestring Fern (sporophyte)

Zamia integrifolia Florida Coontie

 CANDLER

Astragalis michauxii Sandhill Milkvetch

Balduina atropurpurea Purple Honeycomb Head*

Calamintha ashei Ohoopee Dunes Wild Basil*

Ceratiola ericoides Rosemary*

Cirsium virginianum Virginia Thistle

Elliottia racemosa Georgia Plume*

Epidendrum conopseum Green-fly Orchid*

Hypericum sp.3 Georgia St. Johnswort

Lachnocaulon beyrichianum Southern Bog-button

Liatris pauciflora Few-flower Gay-feather

Platanthera nivea Snowy Orchid

Rhynochospora culixa Georgia Beaksedge

Sarracenia flava Yellow Flytrap*

Sarracenia minor Hooded Pitcherplant*

Sarracenia psittacina Parrot Pitcherplant*

Sarracenia rubra Sweet Pitcherplant†

Sideroxylon sp.1 Ohoopee Bumelia

Sporobolus teretifolius Wire-leaf Dropseed

Stewartia malacodendron Silky Camellia*

 CARROLL

Hexastylis shuttleworthii var. harperi Harper Heartleaf*

Platanthera integrilabia Monkeyface Orchid†

Schisandra glabra Bay Starvine*

Waldsteinia lobata Piedmont Barren Strawberry*

 CATOOSA

Asplenium ruta-muraria Wall Rue Spleenwort

Astranthium integrifolium Wild Daisy

Baptisia australis var. aberrans Glade Blue Indigo

Bouteloua curtipendula Side-oats Grama

Buchnera americana Bluehearts

Camassia scilloides Wild Hyacinth

Dalea candida Prairie Clover

Dalea gattingeri Gattinger Prairie Clover

Delphinium carolinianum ssp. calciphilum Glade Larkspur

Eleocharis compressa Spikerush

Erigenia bulbosa Harbinger-of-spring

Fraxinus quadrangulata Blue Ash

Helianthus occidentalis Barrens Sunflower

Heliotropium tenellum Delicate Heliotrope

Hypericum dolabriforme Glade St. Johnswort

Isoetes butleri Glade Quillwort

Juncus filipendulus Texas Plains Rush

Leavenworthia exigua var. exigua Gladecress*

Liatris squarrosa var. hirsute Glade Gay-feather

Matelea obliqua Limerock Milkvine

Mertensia virginica Virginia Bluebells

Onosmodium molle ssp. occidentale Marble-seed

Ophioglossum engelmannii Limestone Adder-tongue Fern

Parnassia grandiflora Largeleaf Grass-of-Parnassus

Pediomelum subacaule Nashville Breadroot

Polemonium reptans Jacob's Ladder

Rudbeckia grandiflora Largeflower Coneflower

Scutellaria leonardii Glade Skullcap

Scutellaria montana Large-flowered Skullcap†

Silphium radula Rosinweed

Spiranthes magnicamporum Great Plains Ladies-tresses*

Sporobolus heterolepis Prairie Dropseed

Symphyotrichum pratense Silky Aster

Thaspium pinnatifidum Cutleaf Meadow-parsnip

Viola egglestonii Glade Violet

CHARLTON

Aeschynomene viscidula Sticky Joint-vetch

Agalinis aphylla Scale-leaf Purple Foxglove

Asclepias pedicellata Savanna Milkweed

Asimina pygmaea Dwarf Pawpaw

Baldiuna atropurpurea Purple Honeycomb Head*

Ctenium floridanum Florida Orange-grass

Fuirena scirpoidea Southern Umbrella-sedge

Galactia floridana Florida Milk-pea

Gymnopogon chapmanianus Chapman Skeleton Grass

Hartwrightia floridana Hartwrightia*

Lachnocaulon beyrichianum Southern Bog-button

Litsea aestivalis Pondspice*

Peltandra sagittifolia Arrow Arum

Piloblephis rigida Pennyroyal

Plantago sparsiflora Pineland Plantain

Platanthera integra Yellow Fringeless Orchid

Psilotum nudum Whisk Fern

Quercus chapmanii Chapman Oak

Rhynchospora alba Northern White Beaksedge

Sarracenia flava Yellow Flytrap*

Sarracenia minor Hooded Pitcherplant*

Sarracenia psittacina Parrot Pitcherplant*

Sideroxylon alachuense Silver Buckthorn

Spiranthes floridana Florida Ladies-tresses

Tephrosia chrysophylla Sprawling Goats Rue

Tillandsia bartramii Bartram's Air-plant

CHATHAM

Forestiera segregata Florida Privet

Hibiscus grandiflorus Swamp Hibiscus

Lindera melissifolia Pondberry†

Physostegia leptophylla Tidal Marsh Obedient Plant*

Rhynchospora punctata Pineland Beaksedge

Sapindus saponaria Soapberry

Sarracenia minor Hooded Pitcherplant*

Scutellaria mellichampii Skullcap

Sporobolus pinetorum Pineland Dropseed

Vigna luteola Wild Yellow Cowpea

CHATTAHOOCHE

Aeculus parviflora Bottlebrush Buckeye

Arabis georgiana Georgia Rockcress†

Brickellia cordifolia Flyr's Nemesis

Carex stricta Tussock Sedge

Croomia pauciflora Croomia*

Desmodium sessilifolium Sessile-leaf Tick-trefoil

Gymnopogon brevifolius Broad-leaved
Beardgrass

Helenium brevifolium Bog Sneezeweed

Helianthemum canadense Canadian
Frostweed

Hexastylis shuttleworthii var. harperi
Harper Heartleaf*

Iris brevicaulis Lamance Iris

Melanthium latifolium Broadleaf
Bunchflower

Mirabilis albida Pale Umbrella-wort

Myriophyllum laxum Lax Water-milfoil*

Oldenlandia boscii Bluets

Panax quinquefolius American Ginseng

Phaseolus polystachios var. sinuatus
Trailing Bean-vine

Quercus arkansana Arkansas Oak

Quercus prinoides Dwarf Chinkapin Oak

Rhododendron prunifolium Plumleaf
Azalea*

Schisandra glabra Bay Starvine*

Stylisma pickeringii var. pickeringii
Pickering Morning Glory*

Tragia cordata Heartleaf Nettle Vine

Trepocarpus aethusae Trepocarpus

Triadenum tubulosum Broadleaf Marsh
St. Johnswort

Tridens carolinianus Carolina Redtop

CHATTOOGA

Aster georgianus Georgia Aster†

Carex purpurifera Purple Sedge*

Cypripedium acaule Pink Lady's Slipper*

Pachysandra procumbens Allegheny-
spurge

Panax quinquefolius American Ginseng

Phlox amplifolia Broadleaf Phlox

Plantanthera integrilabia Monkeyface
Orchid†

Rudbeckia heliopsidis Little River Black-
eyed Susan

Sagittaria secundifolia Little River Water-
plantain†

Scutellaria montana Large-flowered
Skullcap†

Scutellaria nervosa Bottomland Skullcap

Stachys nuttallii Nuttall's Hedge-nettle

CHEROKEE

Lygodium palmatum Climbing
Fern

Lysimachia fraseri Fraser Loosestrife*

Nestronia umbellula Indian Olive*

Prunus virginiana Chokecherry

Schusandra glabra Bay Starvine*

Xerophyllum asphodeloides Eastern
Turkeybeard*

CLARKE

Anemone berlandieri Glade
Windflower

Aster georgianus Georgia Aster†

Draba aprica Open-ground Whitlow-
grass*

Eriocaulon koernickianum Dwarf
Pipewort

Melanthium latifolium Broadleaf
Bunchflower

Nestronia umbellula Indian Olive*

Sedum pusillum Granite Stonecrop*

CLAY

Aesculus parviflora Bottlebrush
Buckeye

Anemone berlandieri Glade Windflower

Arabis georgiana Georgia Rockcress*

Baptisia megacarpa Bigpod Wild Indigo

Brickellia cordifolia Flyr's Nemesis

Croomia pauciflora Croomia*

Matelea alabamensis Alabama Milkvine*

Melanthium woodii Ozark Bunchflower*

Panax quiquefolius American Ginseng

Quercus arkansana Arkansas Oak

Rhododendron prunifolium Plumleaf
Azalea*
Silene ovata Mountain Catchfly
Trepocarpus aethusae Trepocarpus
Trillium reliquum Relict Trillium†

 CLAYTON
Cypripedium acaule Pink Lady's
Slipper*

 CLINCH
Asimina pygmaea Dwarf
Pawpaw
Calopogon multiflorus Many-flowered
Grass-pink
Ctenium floridanum Florida Orange-grass
Fuirena scirpoidea Southern Umbrella-
sedge
Myriophyllum laxum Lax Water-milfoil*
Psilotum nudum Whisk Fern
Sarracenia flava Yellow Flytrap*
Sarracenia minor Hooded Pitcherplant*
Sarracenia psittacina Parrot
Pitcherplant*

 COBB
Arabis missouriensis Missouri
Rockcress
Aster georgianus Georgia Aster†
Calystegia catesbeiana ssp. sericata
Silky Bindweed
Cypripedium acaule Pink Lady's Slipper*
Draba aprica Open-ground Whitlow-
grass*
Melanthium latifolium Broadleaf
Bunchflower
Nestronia umbellula Indian Olive*
Plantanthera integrilabia Monkeyface
Orchid†
Pycnanthemum curvipes Stone
Mountain Mint
Rhus michauxii Dwarf Sumac†

Schisandra glabra Bay Starvine*
Zanthoxylum americanum Northern
Prickly-ash

 COFFEE
Agalinis aphylla Scale-leaf
Purple Foxglove
Baldiuna atropurpurea Purple
Honeycomb Head*
Brachymenium systylium Mexican
Brachymenium
Campylopus carolinae Sandhill Awned
Moss
Elliottia racemosa Georgia Plume*
Epidendrum conopseum Green-fly
Orchid*
Gymnocolea inflata A Liverwort
***Habenaria quinqueseta var. quinque-
seta*** Michaux Orchid
Isoetes melanopoda Black-footed
Quillwort
Marshallia ramosa Pineland Barbara
Buttons*
Oxypolis ternata Savanna Cowbane
Penstemon dissectus Grit Beardtongue*
Portulaca biloba Grit Portulaca
Portulaca umbraticola ssp. coronata
Wingpod Purslane
Rhynchospora macra Southern White
Beaksedge
Rhynchospora punctata Pineland
Beaksedge
Sarracenia flava Yellow Flytrap*
Sarracenia minor Hooded Pitcherplant*
Sarracenia psittacina Parrot
Pitcherplant*
Sporobolus teretifolius Wire-leaf
Dropseed
Trichomanes petersii Dwarf Filmy Fern

COLQUITT

Angelica dentata Sandhill Angelica

Balduina atropurpurea Purple Honeycomb Head*

Drosera tracyi Tracy's Dew-threads

Litsea aestivalis Pondspice*

Myrica inodora Odorless Bayberry

Oxypolis ternata Savanna Cowbane

Plantanthera nivea Snowy Orchid

Rhynchospora solitaria Autumn Beakrush

Sarracenia flava Yellow Flytrap*

Sarracenia minor Hooded Pitcherplant*

Sarracenia psittacina Parrot Pitcherplant*

Sporobolus teretifolius Wire-leaf Dropseed

Stokesia laevis Stokes Aster

 COLUMBIA

Amorpha georgiana var. georgiana Georgia Indigo-bush

Amphianthus pusillus Pool Sprite†

Anemone berlandieri Glade Windflower

Arabis missouriensis Missouri Rockcress

Aster georgianus Georgia Aster†

Bouteloua curtipendula Side-oats Grama

Clematis ochroleuca Curly-heads

Draba aprica Open-ground Whitlow-grass*

Dryopteris celsa Log Fern

Elliottia racemosa Georgia Plume*

Hymenocallis coronaria Shoals Spiderlily*

Isoetes tegetiformans Mat-forming Quillwort†

Marshallia ramosa Pineland Barbara Buttons*

Paronychia virginica Yellow Nailwort

Pediumelum sp.2 Dixie Mountain Breadroot

Portulaca umbraticola ssp. coronata Wingpod Purslane

Scutellaria ocmulgee Ocmulgee Skullcap*

Sedum pusillum Granite Stonecrop*

Trillium reliquum Relict Trillium†

 COOK

Angelica dentata Sandhill Angelica

Balduina atropurpurea Purple Honeycomb Head*

Dalea carnea var. gracilis Sprawling White-tassels

Drosera tracyi Tracy's Dew-threads

Macbridea caroliniana Carolina Bogmint

Sarracenia flava Yellow Flytrap*

Sarracenia minor Hooded Pitcherplant*

Sporobolus teretifolius Wire-leaf Dropseed

Stewartia malacodendron Silky Camellia*

 COWETA

Cypripedium acaule Pink Lady's Slipper*

Platanthera integrilabia Monkeyface Orchid†

Schisandra glabra Bay Starvine*

 CRAWFORD

Chamaecyparis thyoides Atlantic White-cedar*

Sarracenia rubra Sweet Pitcherplant†

Scirpus etuberculatus Canby's Club-rush

Silene polypetala Fringed Campion†

 CRISP

Macranthera flammea Flame Flower

Penstemon dissectus Grit Beardtongue*

Ponthieva racemosa Shadow-witch Orchid

Rhexia aristosa Awned Meadowbeauty

Sarracenia flava Yellow Flytrap*
Sarracenia minor Hooded Pitcherplant*
Sarracenia psittacina Parrot
  Pitcherplant*
Sideroxylon thornei Swamp Buckthorn*
Sporobolus teretifolius Wire-leaf
  Dropseed

DADE
  Amorpha nitens Shining Indigo-
  bush
Astragalus canadensis Canada Milkvetch
Carex careyana Carey Sedge
Carex purpurifera Purple Sedge*
Cornus drummondii Rough-leaved
  Dogwood
Crataegus triflora Three-flower Hawthorn
Delphinium tricorne Dwarf Larkspur
Dryopteris celsa Log Fern
Helianthus smithii Smith Sunflower
Hypericum sphaerocarpum Barrens St.
  Johnswort
Lathyrus palustris Marsh Wild Pea
Lilium canadense Canada Lily
Lilium philadelphicum Wood Lily
Melanthium woodii Ozark Bunchflower*
Panalamocladium leskeoides A Moss
Saxifraga careyana Carey Saxifrage
Scutellaria montana Large-flowered
  Skullcap†
Silene regia Royal Catchfly*
Silene rotundifolia Roundleaf Catchfly
Silphium mohrii Cumberland Rosinweed
Spiraea virginiana Virginia Spirea†
Trichomanes petersii Dwarf Filmy Fern
Trillium sulcatum Barksdale Trillium

DAWSON
  Aster georgianus Georgia Aster†
Aster phlogifolius Phlox-leaved Aster
Carex manhartii Manhart Sedge*

Cypripendium acaule Pink Lady's
  Slipper*
**Cypripendium parviflorum var. parvi-
  florum** Small-flowered Yellow Lady's
  Slipper*
**Cypripendium parviflorum var. pubes-
  cens** Large-flowered Yellow Lady's
  Slipper*
Hydrastis canadensis Goldenseal*
Juncus gymnocarpus Naked-fruit Rush
Panax trifolius Dwarf Ginseng
Stachys latidens Broad-toothed Hedge-
  nettle
Waldsteinia lobata Piedmont Barren
  Strawberry*
Xerophyllum asphodeloides Eastern
  Turkeybeard*

DECATUR
  Arnoglossum sulcatum
  Grooved-stem Indian-plantain
Aster eryngiifolius Snakeroot-leaf Aster
Aster praealtus Willow-leaf Aster
Baptisia megacarpa Bigpod Wild Indigo
Carex dasycarpa Velvet Sedge*
Carex decomposita Cypress-knee Sedge
Carphephorus pseudoliatris Lavender
  Lady
Chamaecrista deeringiana Florida Senna
Coreopsis integrifolia Tickseed
Crataegus pulcherrima Beautiful Haw
Croomia pauciflora Croomia*
Dalea carnea var. garcilis Sprawling
  White-tassels
Epidendrum conopseum Green-fly
  Orchid*
Illicium floridanum Florida Anise-tree*
Liatris chapmanii Chapman Gay-feather
Litsea aestivalis Pondspice*
Lythrum curtissii Curtiss Loosestrife*
Melanthium woodii Ozark Bunchflower*

Micromeria brownei* var. *pilosiuscula
Savory

Myrica inodora Odorless Bayberry

Myriophyllum laxum Lax Water-milfoil*

Najas filifolia Narrowleaf Naiad

Physostegia leptophylla Tidal Marsh
Obedient Plant*

Platanthera integra Yellow Fringeless
Orchid

Pteroglossaspis ecristata Wild Coco

Schisandra glabra Bay Starvine*

Scirpus erismanae Bulrush

Scirpus etuberculatus Canby's Club-rush

Selanginella ludoviciana Louisiana
Spikemoss

Sideroxylon thornei Swamp Buckthorn*

Silene ovata Mountain Catchfly

Silene polypetala Fringed Campion†

Symphyotrichum pratense Silky Aster

Torreya taxifolia Florida Torreya†

Tragia cordata Heartleaf Nettle Vine

Tridens carolinianus Carolina Redtop

Trillium lancifolium Lanceleaf Trillium

Zephyranthes simpsonii Simpson Rain
Lily

DEKALB

Allium speculae Flatrock Onion*

Amorpha schwerinii Schwerin Indigo-
bush

Amphianthus pusillus Pool Sprite†

Amsonia ludoviciana Louisiana Blue Star

Anemone berlandieri Glade Windflower

Aster avitus Alexander Rock Aster

Aster georgianus Georgia Aster†

Eriocaulon koernickianum Dwarf
Pipewort

Fimbristylis brevivaginata Flatrock
Fimbry

Isoetes melanospora Black-spored
Quillwort†

Melanthium woodii Ozark Bunchflower*

Nestronia umbellula Indian Olive*

Panax quiquefolius American Ginseng

Pilularia americana American Pillwort

Pycnanthemum curvipes Stone
Mountain Mint

Ribes curvatum Granite Gooseberry

Schisandra glabra Bay Starvine*

Sedum pusillum Granite Stonecrop*

***Viburnum rafinesquianum* var.
*rafinesquianum*** Downy Arrowwood

Waldsteinia lobata Piedmont Barren
Strawberry*

DODGE

Astragalus michauxii Sandhill
Milkvetch

Marshallia ramosa Pineland Barbara
Buttons*

Sarracenia flava Yellow Flytrap*

Sarracenia minor Hooded Pitcherplant*

Sporobolus teretifolius Wire-leaf
Dropseed

Stokesia laevis Stokes Aster

DOOLY

Carex decompositia Cypress-
knee Sedge

Lobelia boykinii Boykin Lobelia

Oxypolis canbyii Canby Dropwort†

Ptilimnium nodosum Harperella†

DOUGHTERY

Armoracia lacustris Lake-cress

Epidendrum conopseum Green-fly
Orchid*

Leitneria floridana Corkwood

Listera australis Southern Twayblade

Lobelia boykinii Boykin Lobelia

Plantago sparsiflora Pineland Plantain

Polygala bladuinii White Milkwort

Pteroglossaspis ecristata Wild Coco

Rhexia aristosa Awned Meadowbeauty

Sarracenia minor Hooded Pitcherplant*
Schwalbea americana Chaffseed†
Scirpus hallii Hall Bulrush
Sideroxylon thornei Swamp Buckthorn*
Sium floridanum Florida Water-parsnip
Stylisma pickeringii var. pickeringii Pickering Morning Glory*
Thalictrum cooleyi Cooley Meadowrue†

DOUGLAS
Amphianthus pusillus Pool Sprite
Arabis missouriensis Missouri Rockcress
Cypripedium acaule Pink Lady's Slipper*
Cypripedium parviflorum var. pubescens Large-flowered Lady's Slipper*
Panax quinquefolius American Ginseng
Schisandra glabra Bay Starvine*
Waldsteinia lobata Piedmont Barren Strawberry*

EARLY
Aesculus parviflora Bottlebrush Buckeye
Arnoglossum diversifolium Variable-leaf Indian-plantain*
Arnoglossum sulcatum Grooved-stem Indian-plantain
Brickellia cordofolia Flyr's Nemesis
Carex baltzellii Baltzell Sedge*
Carex dasycarpa Velvet Sedge*
Epidendrum conopseum Green-fly Orchid*
Lythrum curtissii Curtiss Loosestrife*
Macranthera flammea Flame Flower
Matelea alabamensis Alabama Milkvine*
Melanthium woodii Ozark Bunchflower*
Myriophyllum laxum Lax Water-milfoil*
Peltandra sagittifolia Arrow Arum
Pinguicula primulifolia Clearwater Butterwort*
Ponthieva racemosa Shadow-witch Orchid

Quercus arkansana Arkansas Oak
Quercus sinuata Durand Oak
Rhododendron prunifolium Plumleaf Azalea*
Salix floridana Florida Willow*
Sarracenia leucophylla Whitetop Pitcherplant*
Sarracenia minor Hooded Pitcherplant*
Sarracenia psittacina Parrot Pitcherplant*
Sarracenia rubra Sweet Pitcherplant†
Schwalbea americana Chaffseed†
Sideroxylon thornei Swamp Buckthorn*
Tephrosia mohrii Dwarf Goats Rue
Trillium reliquum Relict Trillium†
Utricularia olivacea Leafless Dwarf Bladderwort

ECHOLS
Amorpha herbacea var. floridana Florida Leadbush
Asclepias pedicellata Savanna Milkweed
Batisia lecontei Leconte Wild Indigo
Epidendrum conopseum Green-fly Orchid*
Lachnocaulon beyrichianum Southern Bog-button
Sarracenia flava Yellow Flytrap*

EFFINGHAM
Epidendrum conopseum Green-fly Orchid*
Lachnocaulon beyrichianum Southern Bog-Button
Lindera melissifolia Pondberry†
Listera australis Southern Twayblade
Listea aestivalis Pondspice*
Peltandra sagittifolia Arrow Arum
Sarracenia flava Yellow Flytrap*
Silene caroliniana Carolina Pink
Stewartia malacondendron Silky Camellia*

ELBERT

Clematis ochroleuca Curly-
heads

Juniperus communis var. depressa
Ground Juniper

Lotus helleri Carolina Birdfoot-trefoil

Quercus oglethorpensis Oglethorpe Oak*

Rhus michauxii Dwarf Sumact

Scirpus expansus Woodland Bulrush

Sedum pusillum Granite Stonecrop*

Trillium discolor Pale Yellow Trillium

Trillium lancifolium Lanceleaf Trillium

EMANUEL

Astragalus michauxii
Sandhill Milkvetch

Balduina atropurpurea Purple
Honeycomb Head*

Ceratiola ericoides Rosemary*

Elliottia racemosa Georgia Plume*

Epidendrum conopseum Green-fly
Orchid*

Fothergilla gardenia Dwarf Witch-alder*

Hypericum sp.3 Georgia St. Johnswort

Lachnocaulon beyrichianum Southern
Bog-button

Liatris pauciflora Few-flower Gay-feather

Macranthera flammea Flame Flower

Nestronia umbellula Indian Olive*

Oldenlandia boscii Bluets

Peltandra sagittifolia Arrow Arum

Penstemon dissectus Grit Beardtongue*

Phaseolus polystachios var. sinuatus
Trailing Bean-vine

Platanthera nivea Snowy Orchid

Ponthieva racemosa Shadow-witch
Orchid

Sarracenia flava Yellow Flytrap*

Sarracenia minor Hooded Pitcherplant*

Sarracenia psittacina Parrot
Pitcherplant*

Sideroxylon sp.1 Ohoopee Bumelia

Sporobolus teretifolius Wire-leaf
Dropseed

Stewartia malacodendron Silky
Camellia*

EVANS

Balduina atropurpurea Purple
Honeycomb Head*

Elliottia racemosa Georgia Plume*

Ipomoea macrorhiza Large-stem Morning
Glory

Liatris pauciflora Few-flower Gay-feather

Litsea aestivalis Pondspice*

Lobelia boykinii Boykin Lobelia

Macranthera flammea Flame Flower

Penstemon dissectus Grit Beardtongue*

Sarracenia flava Yellow Flytrap*

Sarracenia minor Hooded Pitcherplant*

Sarracenia purpurea Purple Pitcherplant*

Sideroxylon sp.1 Ohoopee Bumelia

FANNIN

Acer spicatum Mountain Maple

Cardamine dissecta Divided Toothwort
(Blue Ridge populations)

Carex purpurifera Purple Sedge*

Coreopsis latifolia Broadleaf Tickseed

Cymophyllus fraserianus Fraser Sedge*

Cypripedium acaule Pink Lady's Slipper*

***Cypripedium parviflorum var. parvi-
florum*** Small-flowered Yellow Lady's
Slipper*

***Cypripedium parviflorum var. pubes-
cens*** Large-flowered Yellow Lady's
Slipper*

Hydrastis canadensis Goldenseal*

Isotria medeoloides Small Whorled
Pogoniat

Lycopodium clavatum Ground Pine

Melanthium latifolium Broadleaf
Bunchflower

Panax quinquefolius American Ginseng

Panax trifolius Dwarf Ginseng

Platanthera grandiflora Large Purple-fringe Orchid

Platanthera psycodes Small Purple-fringe Orchid

Rhus typhina Staghorn Sumac

Silene ovata Mountain Catchfly

Trillium simile Sweet White Trillium

Triosteum aurantiacum Wild Coffee

Veratrum viride American False Hellebore

Xerophyllum asphodeloides Eastern Turkeybeard*

FAYETTE

Listera australis Southern Twayblade

FLOYD

Amorpha nitens Shining Indigo-bush

Arabis georgiana Georgia Rockcress†

Asclepias hirtella Barrens Milkweed

Asclepias purpurascens Purple Milkweed

Aster novae-angliae New England Aster

Aureolaria patula Spreading Yellow Foxglove

Baptisia australis var. aberrans Glade Blue Indigo

Boltonia caroliniana Carolina Boltonia

Bouteloua curtipendula Side-oats Grama

Buchnera americana Bluehearts

Callirhoe digitata Finger Poppy-mallow

Calystegia catesbeiana ssp. sericata Silky Bindweed

Camassia scilloides Wild Hyacinth

Carex eburnea Black-seed Sedge

Carex purpurifera Purple Sedge*

Carya myristiciformis Nutmeg Hickory

Chaerophyllum procumbens Spreading Chervil

Cheilanthes alabamensis Alabama Lipfern

Cirsium carolinianum Carolina Thistle

Cirsium muticum Swamp Thistle

Clematis fremontii Fremont's Virgin's-bower

Clematis socialis Alabama Leather Flower†

Crataegus triflora Three-flower Hawthorn

Dalea gattingeri Gattinger Prairie Clover

Delphinium tricorne Dwarf Larkspur

Echinacea simulata Prairie Purple Coneflower

Eleocharis compressa Spikerush

Eleocharis tenuis var. verrucosa Warty Slender Spikerush

Erigenia bulbosa Harbinger-of-spring

Erigeron strigosus var calcicola Cedar Glade Daisy Fleabane

Fraxinus quardrangulata Blue Ash

Helianthus verticillatus Whorled Sunflower†

Hypericum dolabriforme Glade St. Johnswort

Hypericum sphaerocarpum Barrens St. Johnswort

Isoetes appalachiana Bigspore Englemann's Quillwort

Isoetes melanopoda Black-footed Quillwort

Jamesianthus alabamensis Jamesianthus

Juncus filipendulus Texas Plains Rush

Liatris squarrosa var. hirsuta Glade Gay-feather

Lilium michiganense Michigan Lily

Marshallia mohrii Coosa Barbara Buttons†

Matelea obliqua Limerock Milkvine

Muhlenbergia sylvatica Woodland Muhly

Oligoneuron riddellii Riddell's Goldenrod

Pachysandra procumbens Allegheny-spurge

Panax quinquefolius American Ginseng

Polemonium reptans Jacob's ladder

Potamogeton amplifolius Bigleaf Pondweed

Prenanthes barbata Flatwoods Rattlesnake-root

Prunus mexicana Mexican Plum

Ptilimnium costatum Eastern Bishopweed

Pycnanthemum virginianum Virginia Mountain-mint

Quercus imbricaria Shingle Oak

Rhynchospora thornei Thorne's Beakrush

Rudbeckia heliopsidis Little River Black-eyed Susan

Sabatia capitata Cumberland Rose Gentian*

Scutellaria leonardii Glade Skullcap

Scutellaria montana Large-flowered Skullcap†

Scutellaria nervosa Bottomland Skullcap

Senecio pauperculus Meadow Golden Ragwort

Silene regia Royal Catchfly*

Spartina pectinata Prairie Cordgrass

Spiranthes magnicamporum Great Plains Ladies-tresses*

Sporobolus heterolepis Prairie Dropseed

Stachys nuttallii Nuttall's Hedge-nettle

Symphyotrichum pratense Silky Aster

Thalictrum debile Trailing Meadowrue*

Trillium lancifolium Lanceleaf Trillium

Ulmus serotina September Elm

Viburnum bracteatum Limerock Arrowwood*

Viburnum rafinesquianum var. affine Limerock Downy Arrowwood

Xyris tennesseesis Tennessee Yellow-eyed Grass†

 FORSYTH

Amorpha nitens Shining Indigo-bush

Amorpha schwerinii Schwerin Indigo-bush

Aster georgianus Georgia Aster†

Platanthera integrilabia Monkeyface Orchid†

 FRANKLIN

Clematis ochroleuca Curly-heads

FULTON

Aster georgianus Georgia Aster†

Cypripedium acaule Pink Lady's Slipper*

Cypripedium parviflorum var. pubescens Large-flowered Yellow Lady's Slipper*

Dryopteris celsa Log Fern

Dryopteris cristata Crested Wood Fern

Fothergilla major Mountain Witch-alder

Hexastylis shuttleworthii var. harperi Harper Heartleaf*

Listera australis Southern Twayblade

Panax quiquefolius American Ginseng

Schisandra glabra Bay Starvine*

Waldsteinia lobata Piedmont Barren Strawberry*

 GILMER

Aster phlogifolius Phlox-leaved Aster

Calystegia catesbeiana ssp. sericata Silky Bindweed

Carex appalachica Appalachian Sedge

Carex manhartii Manhart Sedge*

Carex scabrata Sedge

Coreopsis latifolia Broadleaf Tickseed

Cypripedium acaule Pink Lady's Slipper*

Cypripedium parviflorum var. pubescens Large-flowered Yellow Lady's Slipper*

Heracleum lanatum Masterwort

Isotria medeoloides Small Whorled Pogonia†

Juglans cenerea Butternut (nut-bearing only)

Juncus gymnocarpus Naked-fruit Rush

Lygodium palmatum Climbing Fern

Melanthium latifolium Broadleaf Bunchflower

Panax quiquefolius American Ginseng

Phlox amplifolia Broadleaf Phlox

Platanthera grandiflora Large Purple-fringed Orchid

Prunus virginiana Chokecherry

Sarracenia oreophila Green Pitcherplant†

Trientalis borealis Northern Starflower*

Trillium simile Sweet White Trillium

Triosteum aurantiacum Wild Coffee

Veratrum viride American False Hellebore

GLASCOCK

Zephyranthes simpsonii Simpson Rain Lily

GLYNN

Agalinis divaricata Pineland Purple Foxglove

Asclepias pedicellata Savanna Milkweed

Carex decomposita Cypress-knee Sedge

Coreopsis integrifolia Tickseed

Eleocharis albida White Spikerush

Epidendrum conopseum Green-fly Orchid*

Forestiera segregata Florida Privet

Hibiscus grandiflorus Swamp Hibiscus

Leitneria floridana Corkwood

Litsea aestivalis Pondspice*

Palafoxia integrifolia Palafoxia

Peltandra sagittifolia Arrow Arum

Piloblephis rigida Pennyroyal

Plantago sparsiflora Pineland Plantain

Polygala balduinii White Milkwort

Psilotum nudum Whisk Fern

Quercus austrina Bluff White Oak

Quercus chapmanii Chapman Oak

Sageretia minutiflora Tiny-leaf Buckthorn*

Sarracenia minor Hooded Pitcherplant*

Thalia dealbata Flag

Tillandsia bartramii Bartram's Air-plant

Tillandsia recurvata Ball-moss*

Tillandsia setacea Pine-needle Air-plant

Zamia integrifolia Florida Coontie

GORDON

Amorpha nitens Shining Indigo-bush

Arabis georgiana Georgia Rockcress†

Carex grayi Asa Gray Sedge

Carex purpurifera Purple Sedge*

Chaerophyllum procumbens Spreading Chervil

Delphinium tricorne Dwarf Larkspur

Eleocharis tenuis var. verrucosa Warty Slender Spikerush

Erigenia bulbosa Harbinger-of-spring

Panax quiquefolius American Ginseng

Parietaria pensylvanica Pennsylvania Pellitory

Polemonium reptans Jacob's ladder

Quercus palustris Pin Oak

Sabatia capitata Cumberland Rose Gentian*

Scutellaria montana Large-flowered Skullcap†

Thalictrum debile Trailing Meadowrue*

Trillium lancifolium Lanceleaf Trillium

Xyris tennesseensis Tennessee Yellow-eyed Grass†

GRADY

Angelica dentata Sandhill Angelica

Epidendrum conopseum Green-fly Orchid*

Listera australis Southern Twayblade

Myrica inodora Odorless Bayberry

Tephrosia mohrii Dwarf Goats Rue

Vigna luteola Wild Yellow Cowpea

GREENE

Amorpha schwerinii Schwerin Indigo-bush

Amphianthus pusillus Pool Sprite†

Elatine triandra Longstem Waterwort

Eriocaulon koernickianum Dwarf Pipewort

Isoetes melanospora Black-spored Quillwort†

Isoetes tegetiformans Mat-forming Quillwort†

Panax quiquefolius American Ginseng

Pilularia americana American Pillwort

Ptilimnium nodosum Harperella†

Quercus oglethorpensis Oglethorpe Oak*

Sedum pusillum Granite Stonecrop*

GWINNETT

Aesculus glabra Ohio Buckeye

Amphianthus pusillus Pool Sprite†

Amsonia ludoviciana Louisiana Blue Star

Aster avitus Alexander Rock Aster

Aster georgianus Georgia Aster†

Cypripedium acaule Pink Lady's Slipper*

Cypripedium parviflorum var. pubscens Large-flowered Yellow Lady's Slipper*

Eriocaulon koernickianium Dwarf Pipewort

Fimbristylis brevivaginata Flatrock Fimbry

Hydrasis canadensis Goldenseal*

Isoetes melanospora Black-spored Quillwort†

Melanthium woodii Ozark Bunchflower*

Panax quinquefolius American Ginseng

Schisandra glabra Bay Starvine*

Sedum pusillum Granite Stonecrop*

Waldsteinia lobata Piedmont Barren Strawberry*

HABERSHAM

Aster georgianus Georgia Aster†

Carex albursina White Bear Lake Sedge

Carex scabrata Sedge

Cypripedium acaule Pink Lady's Slipper*

Echinacea laevigata Smooth Purple Coneflower†

Huperzia porophila Rock Clubmoss

Isotria medeoloides Small Whorled Pogonia†

Juncus gymnocarpus Naked-fruit Rush

Lygodium palmatum Climbing Fern

Panax quinquefolius American Ginseng

Parnassia grandifolia Largeleaf Grass-of-Parnassus

Trichomanes petersii Dwarf Filmy Fern

Trillium persisens Persistent Trillium†

Waldsteinia lobata Piedmont Barren Strawberry*

HALL

Hydrastis canadensis Goldenseal*

Melanthium woodii Ozark Bunchflower*

Nestronia umbellula Indian Olive*

Spiraea alba var. latifolia Broadleaf White Spirea

HANCOCK

Amphianthus pusillus Pool Sprite†

Aster avitus Alexander Rock Aster

Elatine triandra Longstem Waterwort

Eriocaulon koernickianum Dwarf
Pipewort

Fimbristylis brevivaginata Flatrock
Fimbry

Isoetes tegetiformans Mat-forming
Quillwort†

Lindera subcoriacea Bog Spicebush

Pilularia americana American Pillwort

Stewartia malacodendron Silky
Camellia*

 HARALSON
***Cypripedium parvoflorum var.
pubescens*** Large-flowered Yellow Lady's
Slipper*

Melanthium woodii Ozark Bunchflower*

Nestronia umbellula Indian Olive*

Pachysandra procumbens Allegheny-
spurge

Trillium lancifolium Lanceleaf Trillium

 HARRIS
Aesculus parviflora Bottlebrush
Buckeye

Amorpha nitens Shining Indigo-bush

Amphianthus pusillus Pool Sprite†

Arabis georgiana Georgia Rockcress†

Croomia pauciflora Croomia*

Hymenocallis coronaria Shoals
Spiderlily*

Listera australis Southern Twayblade

Pachysandra procumbens Allegheny-
spurge

Panax quinquefolius American Ginseng

Rhododendron prunifolium Plumleaf
Azalea*

Sedum nevii Nevius Stonecrop*

Stewartia malacodendron Silky
Camellia*

Trillium reliquum Relict Trillium†

 HART
Trillium discolor Pale Yellow
Trillium

 HEARD
Amphianthus pusillus Pool
Sprite†

Cuscuta harperi Harper Dodder*

***Cypripedium parviflorum var. pubes-
cens*** Large-flowered Yellow Lady's
Slipper*

Isoetes melanospora Black-spored
Quillwort†

Schisandra glabra Bay Starvine*

Waldsteinia lobata Piedmont Barren
Strawberry*

 HENRY
Amphianthus pusillus Pool
Sprite†

Cypripedium acaule Pink Lady's Slipper*

Sedum pusillum Granite Stonecrop*

 HOUSTON
***Hexastylis shuttleworthii var.
harperi*** Harper Heartleaf*

Lobelia boykinii Boykin Lobelia

Rhexia aristosa Awned Meadowbeauty

Scutellaria ocmulgee Ocmulgee
Skullcap*

Teloschistes exilis Orange Fructicose Bark
Lichen

Tragia cordata Heartleaf Nettle Vine

Trillium lancifolium Lanceleaf Trillium

Trillium reliquum Relict Trillium†

 IRWIN
Agalinis aphylla Scale-leaf
Purple Foxglove

Andropogon mohrii Bog Bluestem

Balduina atropurpurea Purple
Honeycomb Head*

Elliottia racemosa Georgia Plume*
Lobelia boykinii Boykin Lobelia
Myriophyllum laxum Lax Water-milfoil*
Plantanthera integra Yellow Fringeless Orchid
Sarracenia flava Yellow Flytrap*
Sarracenia minor Hooded Pitcherplant*
Sarracenia psittacina Parrot Pitcherplant*
Stewartia malacodendron Silky Camellia*

JACKSON
Amphianthus pusillus Pool Sprite†
Isoetes melandospora Black-spored Quillwort†
Isoetes tegetiformans Mat-forming Quillwort†

JASPER
Anemone caroliniana Carolina Windflower
Cypripedium acaule Pink Lady's Slipper*
Dryopteris celsa Log Fern
Listera australis Southern Twayblade
Quercus oglethorpensis Oglethorpe Oak*

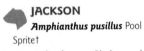
JEFF DAVIS
Balduina atropurpurea Purple Honeycomb Head*
Elliottia racemosa Georgia Plume*
Epidendrum conopseum Green-fly Orchid*
Iris tridentata Savanna Iris
Isoetes appalachiana Bigspore Engelmann's Quillwort
Marshallia ramosa Pineland Barbara Buttons*
Oxypolis ternata Savanna Cowbane
Penstemon dissectus Grit Beardtongue*
Polygala leptostachys Georgia Milkwort

Portulaca biloba Grit Portulaca
Quercus austrina Bluff White Oak
Rhynospora punctata Pineland Beaksedge
Sarracenia flava Yellow Flytrap*
Sarracenia minor Hooded Pitcherplant*
Sarracenia psittacina Parrot Pitcherplant*
Sideroxylon sp.1 Ohoopee Bumelia
Sporobolus teretifolius Wire-leaf Dropseed

JEFFERSON
Nestronia umbellula Indian Olive*
Penstemon dissectus Grit Beardtongue*
Sarracenia rubra Sweet Pitcherplant†

JENKINS
Astragalus michauxii Sandhill Milkvetch
Lobelia boykinii Boykin Lobelia
Malaxis spicata Florida Adders-mouth
Oxypolis Canbyi Canby Dropwort†
Rhexia aristosa Awned Meadowbeauty
Sarracenia flava Yellow Flytrap*
Silene caroliniana Carolina Pink
Stylisma pickeringii var. pickeringii Pickering Morning Glory*

JOHNSON
Marshallia ramosa Pineland Barbara Buttons*
Penstemon *dissectus* Grit Beardtongue*
Portulaca biloba Grit Portulaca
Sarracenia flava Yellow Flytrap*

JONES
Lindera subcoriacea Bog Spicebush
Nestronia umbellula Indian Olive*
Trillium reliquum Relict Trillium†

LAMAR
No endangered plants listed in Lamar County, Georgia.

LANIER
Asimina reticulata Netleaf Pawpaw
Baptisia lecontei Leconte Wild Indigo
Epidendrum conopseum Green-fly Orchid*
Sarracenia flava Yellow Flytrap*
Sarracenia minor Hooded Pitcherplant*
Sarracenia psittacina Parrot Pitcherplant*
Xyris scabrifolia Harper Yellow-eyed Grass

LAURENS
Astralus michauxii Sandhill Milkvetch
Cypripedium kentuckiense Kentucky Lady's Slipper
Isoetes boomii Boom Quillwort
Marshallia ramosa Pineland Barbara Buttons*
Penstemon dissectus Grit Beardtongue*
Sarracenia flava Yellow Flytrap*
Sarracenia minor Hooded Pitcherplant*
Scutellaria mellichampii Skullcap
Scutellaria ocmulgee Ocmulgee Skullcap*
Sideroxylon sp. I Ohoopee Burmelia
Sideroxylon thornei Swamp Buckthorn*
Tillandsia setacea Pine-needle Air-plant
Trillium reliquum Relict Trillium†

LEE
Arnoglossum sulcatum Grooved-stem Indian-plantain
Asplenium heteroresiliens Wagner Spleenwort*
Desmodium ochroleucum Creamflower Tick-trefoil

Lobelia boykinii Boykin Lobelia
Oldenlandia boscii Bluets
Oxypolis canbyi Canby Dropwort†
Plantago sparsiflora Pineland Plantain
Rhexia aristosa Awned Meadowbeauty
Sarracenia leucophylla Whitetop Pitcherplant*
Sarracenia minor Hooded Pitcherplant*
Sideroxylon thornei Swamp Buckthorn*
Stewartia malacondendron Silky Camellia*
Tragia cordata Heartleaf Nettle Vine
Trillium reliquum Relict Trillium†

LIBERTY
Agalinis aphylla Scale-leaf Purple Foxglove
Balduina atropurpurea Purple Honeycomb Head*
Carex dasycarpa Velvet Sedge*
Eleocharis montevidensis Spikerush
Epidendrum conopseum Green-fly Orchid*
Habenaria quinqueseta var. quinqueseta Michaux Orchid
Lobelia boykinii Boykin Lobelia
Pteroglossaspis ecristata Wild Coco
Quercus chapmanii Chapman Oak
Rhynchospora torreyana Torrey Beakrush
Sapindus saponaria Soapberry
Sarracenia minor Hooded Pitcherplant*
Scutellaria mellichampii Skullcap
Sideroxylon thornei Swamp Buckthorn*
Sporobolus pinetorum Pineland Dropseed
Stewartia malacodendron Silky Camellia*

LINCOLN

Amorpha schwerinii Schwerin Indigo-bush

Hymenocallis coronaria Shoals Spiderlily*

Lotus helleri Carolina Birdfoot-trefoil

LONG

Balduina atropurpurea Purple Honeycomb Head*

Calopogon multiflorus Many-flowered Grass-pink

Carex dasycarpa Velvet Sedge*

Dalea feayi Feay Pink-tassels

Elliottia racemosa Georgia Plume*

Epidendrum conopseum Green-fly Orchid*

Fothergilla gardenii Dwarf Witch-alder*

Ilex amelanchier Serviceberry Holly

Ipomoea macrorhiza Large-stem Morning Glory

Liatris pauciflora Few-flower Gay-feather

Litsea aestivalis Pondspice*

Lobelia boykinii Boykin Lobelia

Matelea Pubiflora Trailing Milkvine*

Peltandra sagittifolia Arrow Arum

Penstemon dissectus Grit Beardtongue*

Plantago sparsiflora Pineland Plantain

Platanthera nivea Snowy Orchid

Pteroglossaspis ecristata Wild Coco

Quercus austrina Bluff White Oak

Sarracenia flava Yellow Flytrap*

Sarracenia minor Hooded Pitcherplant*

Sideroxylon sp. I Ohoopee Bumelia

Sporobolus pinetorum Pineland Dropseed

LOWNDES

Agalinis aphylla Scale-leaf Purple Foxglove

Baptisia lecontei Leconte Wild Indigo

Drosera tracyi Tracy's Dew-threads

Epidendrum conopseum Green-fly Orchid*

Fuirena scirpoidea Southern Umbrella-sedge

Lachnocaulon beyrichianum Southern Bog-button

Lobelia boykinii Boykin Lobelia

Macbridea caroliniana Carolina Bogmint

Oxypolis ternata Savanna Cowbane

Polygala leptostachys Georgia Milkwort

Quercus austrina Bluff White Oak

Sarracenia flava Yellow Flytrap*

Sarracenia minor Hooded Pitcherplant*

LUMPKIN

Aster phlogifolius Phlox-leaved Aster

Calycanthus brockiana Brock Sweetshrub

Calystegia catesbeiana ssp. sericata Silky Bindweed

Carex appalachica Appalachian Sedge

Sarracenia manhartii Manhart Sedge*

Carex scabrata Sedge

*Corydalis sem*pervirens Pale Corydalis

Cypripedium acaule Pink Lady's Slipper*

Cypripedium parviflorum var. pubescens Large-flowered Yellow Lady's Slipper*

Herpetineuron toccoae A Moss

Hypericum buckleii Blue Ridge St. Johnswort

Juncus gymnocarpus Naked-fruit Rush

Paronychia argyrocoma Silverling

Penstemon smallii Small's Beardtongue

Silene ovata Mountain Catchfly

Trillium simile Sweet White Trillium

Xerophyllum asphodeloides Eastern Turkeybeard*

MACON

Cayaponia quiqueloba
Cayaponia

Chamaecyparis thyoides Atlantic White-cedar*

Fothergilla gardenii Dwarf Witch-alder*

Nestronia umbellula Indian Olive*

Quercus arkansana Arkansas Oak

Sarracenia rubra Sweet Pitcherplant†

Scutellaria mellichampii Skullcap

Silene ovata Mountain Catchfly

Tragia cordata Heartleaf Nettle Vine

Triadenum tubulosum Broadleaf Marsh St. Johnswort

Trillium reliquum Relict Trillium†

MADISON

Aster georgianus Georgia Aster†

Hexastylis shuttleworthii var. harperi Harper Heartleaf*

Juniperus communis var. depressa Ground Juniper

Quercus prinoides Dwarf Chinkapin Oak

Tradescantia roseolens Rosy Spiderwort

MARION

Carex collinsii Narrow-fruit Swamp Sedge

Chamaecyparis thyoides Atlantic White-cedar*

Dryopteris celsa Log Fern

Helenium brevifolium Bog Sneezeweed

Macbridea caroliniana Carolina Bogmint

Myriophyllum laxum Lax Water-milfoil*

Nestronia umbellula Indian Olive*

Phaseolus polystachios var. sinuatus Trailing Bean-vine

Pinguicula primuliflora Clearwater Butterwort*

Pityopsis pinifolia Sandhill Golden-aster*

Quercus arkansana Arkansas Oak

Sarracenia rubra Sweet Pitcherplant†

Scirpus etuberculatus Canby's Club-rush

Stylisma pickeringii var. pickeringii Pickering Morning Glory*

Xyris chapmanii Chapman Yellow-eyed Grass

MCDUFFIE

Arabis missouriensis Missouri Rockcress

Aster georgianus Georgia Aster†

Elatine triandra Longstem Waterwort

Macbridea caroliniana Carolina Bogmint

Pilularia americana American Pillwort

Saxifraga texana Texas Saxifrage

MCINTOSH

Acacia farnesiana Sweet Acacia

Aeschynomene viscidula Sticky Joint-vetch

Asclepias pedicellata Savanna Milkweed

Carex dasycarpa Velvet Sedge*

Dalea feayi Feay Pink-tassels

Dicerandra radfordiana Radford Dicerandra

Epidendrum conopseum Green-fly Orchid*

Forestiera segregata Florida Privet

Franklinia alatamaha Franklin Tree

Hibiscus grandiflorus Swamp Hibiscus

Hypericum denticulatum var. denticulatum St. Johnswort

Hypericum sp.3 Georgia St. Johnswort

Leitneria floridana Corkwood

Litsea aestivalis Pondspice*

Matelea pubiflora Trailing Milkvine*

Palafoxia integrifolia Palafoxia

Physostegia leptophylla Tidal Marsh Obedient Plant*

Plantago sparsiflora Pineland Plantain

Polygonum glaucum Sea-beach Knotweed

Pteroglossaspis ecristata Wild Coco

Quercus austrina Bluff White Oak
Quercus chapmanii Chapman Oak
Rhynchospora decurrens Swamp-forest
Beaksedge
Ruellia noctiflora Night-blooming Wild
Petunia
Sageretia minutiflora Tiny-leaf
Buckthorn*
Sapindus saponaria Soapberry
Sarracenia minor Hooded Pitcherplant*
Tephrosia chrysophylla Sprawling Goats
Rue
Tillandsia bartramii Bartram's Air-plant
Vigna luteola Wild Yellow Cowpea

 MERIWETHER
Amphianthus pusillus Pool
Sprite†
Aster avitus Alexander Rock Aster
Berberis canadensis American Barberry
Elatine triandra Longstem Waterwort
Eriocaulon koernickianum Dwarf
Pipewort
Ludwigia spathulata Creeping
Smallflower Seedbox
Smilax leptanthera Catbrier
Xyris scabrifolia Harper Yellow-eyed
Grass

 MILLER
Arnoglossum diversifolium
Variable-leaf Indian-plantain*
Asclepias pedicellata Savanna Milkweed
Epidendrum conopseum Green-fly
Orchid*
Litsea aestivalis Pondspice*
Lobelia boykinii Boykin Lobelia
Lythrum curtissii Curtiss Loosestrife*
Oldenlandia boscii Bluets
Ponthieva racemosa Shadow-witch
Orchid
Schwalbea americana Chaffseed†

Sideroxylon thornei Swamp Buckthorn*

 MITCHELL
Evolvulus sericeus var.
sericeus Creeping Morning Glory*
Sarracenia flava Yellow Flytrap*
Sarracenia minor Hooded Pitcherplant*
Sarracenia psittacina Parrot
Pitcherplant*

 MONROE
Quercus prinoides Dwarf
Chinkapin Oak

 MONTGOMERY
Quercus austrina Bluff White Oak
Sideroxylon sp. I Ohoopee Bumelia

 MORGAN
Cypripedium acaule Pink Lady's
Slipper*
Schisandra glabra Bay Starvine*
Waldsteinia lobata Piedmont Barren
Strawberry*

 MURRAY
Aster georgianus Georgia Aster†
Aureolaria patula Spreading
Yellow Foxglove
Carex appalachica Appalachian Sedge
Carex platyphylla Broadleaf Sedge
Carex purpurifera Purple Sedge*
Carex scabrata Sedge
Chrysosplenium americanum Golden
Saxifage
Coreopsis latifolia Broadleaf Tickseed
Cypripedium parviflorum var. parvi-
florum Small-flowered Yellow Lady's
Slipper*
Dryopteris celsa Log Fern
Erigenia bulbosa Harbinger-of-spring
Hydrastis canadensis Goldenseal*

Hydrophyllum macrophyllum Largeleaf Waterleaf

Hypericum dolabriforme Glade St. Johnswort

Juncus filipendulus Texas Plains Rush

Juncus gymnocarpus Naked-fruit Rush

Leavenworthia uniflora Gladecress

Lonicera dioica Limber Honeysuckle

Melanthium latifolium Broadleaf Bunchflower

Panax quinquefolius American Ginseng

Penstemon smallii Small's Beardtongue

Phlox amplifolia Broadleaf Phlox

Platanthera peramoena Purple Fringeless Orchid

Polymnia laevigata Tennessee Leafcup

Sabatia capitata Cumberland Rose Gentian*

Scutellaria montana Large-flowered Skullcap†

Stachys hispida Hispid Hedge-nettle

Stachys nuttallii Nuttall's Hedge-nettle

Trientalis borealis Northern Starflower*

Xerophyllum asphodeloides Eastern Turkeybeard*

MUSCOGEE

Arabis georgiana Georgia Rockcress†

Baptisia megacarpa Bigpod Wild Indigo

Brickellia cordifolia Flyr's Nemesis

Buchnera americana Bluehearts

Cirsium virginianum Virginia Thistle

Croomia pauciflora Croomia*

Helenium brevifolium Bog Sneezeweed

Helianthus smithii Smith Sunflower

Hymenocallis coronaria Shoals Spiderlily*

Isoetes melanopoda Black-footed Quillwort

Melanthium latifolium Broadleaf Bunchflower

Nestronia umbellula Indian Olive*

Phaseolus polystachios var. sinuatus Trailing Bean-vine

Rhus michauxii Dwarf Sumac†

Rhynchospora scirpoides Long-beak Baldrush

Rudbeckia heliopsidis Little River Black-eyed Susan

Sarracenia rubra Sweet Pitcherplant†

Sedum nevii Nevius Stonecrop*

Sedum pusillium Granite Stonecrop*

Stylisma pickeringii var. pickeringii Pickering Morning Glory*

Tridens carolinianus Carolina Redtop

Trillium reliquum Relict Trillium†

NEWTON

Amphianthus pusillus Pool Sprite†

Aster avitus Alexander Rock Aster

Eriocaulon koernickianum Dwarf Pipewort

Isoetes melanospora Black-spored Quillwort†

Portulaca umbraticola ssp. coronata Wingpod Purslane

Quercus prinoides Dwarf Chinkapin Oak

Rhus michauxii Dwarf Sumac†

OCONEE

No endangered plants listed in Oconee County, Georgia.

OGLETHORPE

Amphianthus pusillus Pool Sprite†

Elatine triandra Longstem Waterwort

Lotus helleri Carolina Birdfoot-trefoil

Nestronia umbellula Indian Olive*

Pilularia americana American Pillwort

Portulaca umbraticola ssp. coronata Wingpod Purslane

Quercus oglethorpensis Oglethorpe Oak*
Sedum pusillium Granite Stonecrop*
Trillium discolor Pale Yellow Trillium

PAULDING
Aster georgianus Georgia Aster†
Cypripedium acaule Pink Lady's Slipper*
Schisandra glabra Bay Starvine*

PEACH
Chamaecrista deeringiana Florida Senna
Chamaecyparis thyoides Atlantic White-cedar*
Nestronia umbellula Indian Olive*
Sarracenia rubra Sweet Pitcherplant†

PICKENS
Aster phlogofolius Phlox-leaved Aster
Stachys eplingii Epling's Hedge-nettle
Waldsteinia lobata Piedmont Barren Strawberry*

PIERCE
Quercus chapmanii Chapman Oak
Sarracenia minor Hooded Pitcherplant*
Sideroxylon sp. I Ohoopee Bumelia

PIKE
Amphianthus pusillus Pool Sprite†
Aster avitus Alexander Rock Aster
Pilularia americana American Pillwort
Schwalbea americana Chaffseed†

POLK
Cypripedium acaule Pink Lady's Slipper*
Lygodium palmatum Climbing Fern

Melanthium woodii Ozark Bunchflower*
Silene ovata Mountain Catchfly
Silene regia Royal Catchfly*
Trichomanes petersii Dwarf Filmy Fern

PULASKI
Rhexia aristosa Awned Meadowbeauty
Salix floridana Florida Willow*
Sideroxylon thornei Swamp Buckthorn*

PUTNAM
Amphianthus pusillus Pool Sprite†
Isoetes tegetiformans Mat-forming Quillwort†
Scutellaria nervosa Bottomland Skullcap

QUITMAN
Aesculus parviflora Bottlebrush Buckeye
Brickellia cordifolia Flyr's Nemesis
Croomia pauciflora Croomia*
Quercus arkansana Arkansas Oak
Rhododendron prunifolium Plumleaf Azalea*

RABUN
Agastache scrophulariifolia Purple Giant Hyssop
Aralia nudicaulis Wild Sarsaparilla
Brachyelytrum septentrionale Northern Shorthusk Grass
Calamagrostis porteri Porter's Reedgrass
Calystegia catesbeiana ssp. sericata Silky Bindweed
Carex aestivaliformis Sedge
Carex appalachica Appalachian Sedge
Carex biltmoreana Biltmore Sedge*
Carex lucorum Southern Fibrous Root Sedge
Carex manhartii Manhart Sedge*

Carex misera Wretched Sedge*
Carex pedunculata Longstalk Sedge
Carex roanensis Roan Mountain Sedge
Carex scabrata Sedge
Cephaloziella obtusilobula Roundleaf Leafy Liverwort
Chelone cuthbertii Cuthbert Turtlehead
Comptonia peregrine Sweet-fern
Corydalis sempervirens Pale Corydalis
Cymophyllus fraserianus Fraser Sedge*
Cypripedium acaule Pink Lady's Slipper*
Cypripedium parviflorum var. parviflorum Small-flowered Yellow Lady's Slipper*
Cypripedium parviflorum var. pubescens Large-flowered Yellow Lady's Slipper*
Diphasiastrum tristachyum Ground Cedar
Drosera rotundifolia Roundleaf Sundew
Gymnoderma lineare Rock Gnome Lichen†
Helianthus smithii Smith Sunflower
Helonias bullata Swamp-pink†
Huperzia appalachiana Fir Clubmoss
Hydrastis canadensis Goldenseal*
Hymenophyllum tayloriae Taylor Filmy Fern
Hypericum buckleii Blue Ridge St. Johnswort
Isotria medeoloides Small Whorled Pogonia†
Juglans cinerea Butternut (nut-bearing only)
Juncus gymnocarpus Naked-fruit Rush
Kalmia Carolina Carolina Bog Myrtle
Leiophyllum buxifolium Sand-myrtle
Lejeunea blomquistii Blomquist Leafy Liverwort
Lindernia saxicola Rock False Pimpernel*
Listera smallii Appalachian Twayblade
Lycopodium clavatum Ground Pine

Lygodium palmatum Climbing Fern
Lysimachia fraseri Fraser Loosestrife*
Melanthium latifolium Broadleaf Bunchflower
Menziesia pilosa Minniebush
Panax quinquefolius American Ginseng
Panax trifolius Dwarf Ginseng
Parnassia grandifolia Largeleaf Grass-of-Parnassus
Plagiochila caduciloba Gorge Leafy Liverwort
Plagiochila sharpii Sharp's Leafy Liverwort
Plagiochila sullivantii Sullivant's Leafy Liverwort
Plagiomnium carolinianum Mountain Wavy-leaf Moss
Platanthera integrilabia Monkeyface Orchid†
Platyhypnidium pringlei Pringle's Platyhypnidium
Prunus pensylvanica Fire Cherry
Sanguisorba canadensis Canada Burnet*
Sarracenia purpurea Purple Pitcherplant*
Senecio millefolium Blue Ridge Golden Ragwort*
Shortia galacifolia Oconee Bells*
Solidago simulans Cliffside Goldenrod
Sorbus americana American Mountain-ash
Tofieldia glutinosa Sticky False Asphodel
Trillium persistens Persistant Trillium†
Tsuga caroliniana Carolina Hemlock
Vaccinium erythrocarpum Bearberry
Xerophyllum asphodeloides Eastern Turkeybeard*

RANDOLF

Aster georgianus Georgia Aster†
Brickellia cordifolia Flyr's Nemesis
Linium sulcatum var. harperi Harper Grooved Flax

Panax quinquefolius American Ginseng

Quercus arkansana Arkansas Oak

Rhododendron prunifolium Plumleaf Azalea*

Sarracenia purpurea Purple Pitcherplant*

Silene regia Royal Catchfly*

Thaspium chapmanii Creamy Meadow-parsnip

Tragia cordata Heartleaf Nettle Vine

RICHMOND

Aster georgianus Georgia Aster†

Astragalus michauxii Sandhill Milkvetch

Chamaecyparis thyoides Atlantic White-cedar*

Cypripedium acaule Pink Lady's Slipper*

Hymenocallis coronaria Shoals Spiderlily*

Lindera subcoriacea Bog Spicebush

Nestronia umbellula Indian Olive*

Sarracenia rubra Sweet Pitcherplant†

Scutellaria ocmulgee Ocmulgee Skullcap*

Stewartia malacodendron Silky Camellia*

Stylisma pickeringii var. pickeringii Pickering Morning Glory*

ROCKDALE

Allium speculae Flatrock Onion*

Amphianthus pusillus Pool Sprite†

Amsonia ludoviciana Lousiana Blue Star

Anemone berlandieri Glade Windflower

Aster avitus Alexander Rock Aster

Aster georgianus Georgia Aster†

Cypripedium acaule Pink Lady's Slipper*

Draba aprica Open-ground Whitlow-grass*

Eriocaulon koernickianum Dwarf Pipewort

Fimbristylis brevivaginata Flatrock Fimbry

Isoetes melanospora Black-spored Quillwort†

Portulaca umbraticola ssp. coronata Wingpod Purslane

Sedum pusillum Granite Stonecrop*

SCHLEY

Chamaecyparis thyoides Atlantic White-cedar*

Myriophyllum laxum Lax Water-milfoil*

Pityopsis pinifolia Sandhill Golden-aster*

Ptilimnium nodosum Harperella†

SCREVEN

Astragalus michauxii Sandhill Milkvetch

Hypericum sp.3 Georgia St. Johnswort

Lindera melissifolia Pondberry†

Litsea aestivalis Pondspice*

Oxypolis canbyii Canby Dropwort†

Quercus arkansana Arkansas Oak

Sarracenia minor Hooded Pitcherplant*

Silene caroliniana Carolina Pink

Sporobolus teretifolius Wire-leaf Dropseed

Stewartia malacodendron Silky Camellia*

SEMINOLE

Amorpha nitens Shining Indigo-bush

Brickellia cordifolia Flyr's Nemesis

Carex decomposita Cypress-knee Sedge

Fimbristylis perpusilla Harper Fimbry*

Myriophyllum laxum Lax Water-milfoil*

Sarracenia leucophylla Whitetop Pitcherplant*

Sideroxylon thornei Swamp Buckthorn*

SPALDING

Aster avitus Alexander Rock Aster

STEPHENS

Aster georgianus Georgia Aster†
Carex radfordii Radford Sedge
Cirsium carolinianum Carolina Thistle
Clematis ochroleuca Curly-heads
Echinacea laevigata Smooth Purple
  Coneflower†
Helianthus smithii Smith Sunflower
Lysimachia fraseri Fraser Loosestrife*
Melanthium latifolium Broadleaf
  Bunchflower
Nestronia umbellula Indian Olive*
Panax quinquefolius American Ginseng
Plagiomnium carolinianum Mountain
  Wavy-leaf Moss
Plantanthera integrilabia Monkeyface
  Orchid†
Schisandra glabra Bay Starvine*
Stachys eplingii Epling's Hedge-nettle
Trichomanes petersii Dwarf Filmy Fern
Trillium discolor Pale Yellow Trillium
Waldsteinia lobata Piedmont Barren
  Strawberry*

STEWART

Aesculus parviflora Bottlebrush
  Buckeye
Arabis georgiana Georgia Rockcress†
Parietaria pensylvanica Pennsylvania
  Pellitory
Quercus arkansana Arkansas Oak
Rhododendron prunifolium Plumleaf
  Azalea*
Scirpus etuberculatus Canby's Club-rush
Warea sessilifolia Sandhill-cress

SUMTER

Carex fissa var. aristata Sedge
Fimbristylis perpusilla Harper Fimbry*
Hexastylis shuttleworthii var. harperi
  Harper Heartleaf*
Hypericum adpressum Bog St. Johnswort

Linum sulcatum var. harperi Harper
  Grooved Flax
Oxypolis canbyi Canby Dropwort†
Rhexia aristosa Awned Meadowbeauty
Sarracenia leucophylla Whitetop
  Pitcherplant*
Sarracenia psittacina Parrot
  Pitcherplant*
Sarracenia rubra Sweet Pitcherplant†
Sideroxylon thornei Swamp Buckthorn*

TALBOT

Chamaecyparis thyoides Atlantic
  White-cedar*
Croomia pauciflora Croomia*
Helenium brevifolium Bog Sneezeweed
Hymenocallis coronaria Shoals
  Spiderlily*
Listera australis Southern Twayblade
Myriophyllum laxum Lax Water-milfoil*
Panax quinquefolius American Ginseng
Pityopsis pinifolia Sandhill Golden-aster*
Sarracenia rubra Sweet Pitcherplant†
Silene polypetala Fringed Campion†
Stylisma pickeringii var. pickeringii
  Pickering Morning Glory*
Trillium reliquum Relict Trillium†

TALIAFERRO

No endangered plants listed in
Taliaferro County, Georgia.

TATTNALL

Agalinis aphylla Scale-leaf
  Purple Foxglove
Astragalus michauxii Sandhill Milkvetch
Balduina atropurpurea Purple
  Honeycomb Head*
Calamintha ashei Dunes Wild Basil*
Carex reniformis Reniform Sedge
Ceratiola ericoides Rosemary*
Elliottia racemosa Georgia Plume*

Epidendrum conopseum Green-fly
  Orchid*
Fothergilla gardenia Dwarf Witch-alder*
Hypericum sp.3 Georgia St. Johnswort
Ilex amelanchier Serviceberry Holly
Lechea deckertii Deckert Pinweed
Liatris pauciflora Few-flower Gay-feather
Macranthera flammea Flame Flower
Marshallia ramosa Pineland Barbara
  Buttons*
Matelea pubiflora Trailing Milkvine*
Peltandra sagittifolia Arrow Arum
Penstemon dissectus Grit Beardtongue*
Pteroglossaspis ecristata Wild Coco
Quercus austrina Bluff White Oak
Sarracenia flava Yellow Flytrap*
Sarracenia minor Hooded Pitcherplant*
Sarracenia purpurea Purple Pitcherplant*
Sarracenia rubra Sweet Pitcherplant†
Sideroxylong sp.1 Ohoopee Bumelia
Sideroxylon thornei Swamp Buckthorn*
Stylisma pickeringii var. pickeringii
  Pickering Morning Glory*

TAYLOR
Carex collinsii Narrow-fruit
  Swamp Sedge
Chamaecrista deeringiana Florida Senna
Chamaecyparis thyoides Atlantic White-
  cedar*
Eriophorum virginicum Tawny Cotton-
  grass
Fothergilla gardenii Dwarf Witch-alder*
Helenium brevifolium Bog Sneezeweed
Hexastylis shuttleworthii var. harperi
  Harper Heartleaf*
Kalmia Carolina Carolina Bog Myrtle
Listeria australis Southern Twayblade
Myriophyllum laxum Lax Water-milfoil*
Pachsandra procumbens Allegheny-
  spurge

Pinguicula primuliflora Clearwater
  Butterwort*
Pityopsis pinifolia Sandhill Golden-aster*
Rhynchospora stenophylla Chapman's
  Beakrush
Sarracenia oreophila Green Pitcherplant†
Sarracenia rubra Sweet Pitcherplant†
Scirpus etuberculatus Canby's Club-rush
Silene polypetala Fringed Campion†
Stylisma pickeringii var. pickeringii
  Pickering Morning Glory*

TELFAIR
***Amorpha georgiana var. geor-
giana*** Georgia Indigo-bush
Elliottia racemosa Georgia Plume*
Marshallia ramosa Pineland Barbara
  Buttons*
Penstemon dissectus Grit Beardtongue*
Sarracenia flava Yellow Flytrap*
Sarracenia minor Hooded Pitcherplant*
Sarracenia psittacina Parrot
  Pitcherplant*
Sideroxylon thornei Swamp Buckthorn*
Sporobolus teretifolius Wire-leaf
  Dropseed

TERRELL
Lobelia boykinii Boykin Lobelia
Sideroxylon thornei Swamp Buckthorn*

THOMAS
Angelica dentata Sandhill
  Angelica
Asclepias pedicellata Savanna Milkweed
Calopogon multiflorus Many-flowered
  Grass-pink
Drosera tracyi Tracy's Dew-threads
Liatris tenuifolia var. quadriflora
  Blazing Star
Macranthera flammea Flame Flower
Oxypolis ternata Savanna Cowbane

Platanthera integra Yellow Fringeless
  Orchid
Sarracenia flava Yellow Flytrap*
Sarracenia minor Hooded Pitcherplant*
Sarracenia psittacina Parrot
  Pitcherplant*
Sporobolus teretifolius Wire-leaf
  Dropseed
Stachys hyssopifolia var. lythroides
  Tallahassee Hedge-nettle

TIFT

Andropogon mohrii Bog Bluestem
Balduina atropurpurea Purple
  Honeycomb Head*
Elyonurus tripsacoides Pan-american
  Balsamscale
Isoetes junciformis Rush Quillwort
Oxypolis ternata Savanna Cowbane
Rhynochospora culixa Georgia
  Beaksedge
Rhynochospora solitaria Autumn
  Beakrush
Sarracenia flava Yellow Flytrap*
Sarracenia minor Hooded Pitcherplant*
Sarracenia psittacina Parrot
  Pitcherplant*
Sarracenia purpurea Purple Pitcherplant*
Sporobolus teretifolius Wire-leaf
  Dropseed

TOOMBS

Balduina atropurpurea Purple
  Honeycomb Head*
Ceratiola ericoides Rosemary*
Matelea pubiflora Trailing Milkvine*
Oxypolis ternata Savanna Cowbane
Penstemon dissectus Grit Beardtongue*
Quercus austrina Bluff White Oak
Sarracenia flava Yellow Flytrap*
Sarracenia minor Hooded Pitcherplant*

Sarracenia psittacina Parrot
  Pitcherplant*
Sideroxylon sp. I Ohoopee Burmelia
Sporobolus teretifolius Wire-leaf
  Dropseed

TOWNS

Acer spicatum Mountain Maple
Amelanchier sanguinea Roundleaf
  Serviceberry
Aralia nudicaulis Wild Sarsaparilla
Berberis canadensis American Bayberry
Buchnera americana Bluehearts
Calystegia catesbeiana ssp. sericata
  Silky Bindweed
Carex albursina White Bear Lake Sedge
Carex appalachica Appalachian Sedge
Carex biltmoreana Biltmore Sedge*
Carex manhartii Manhart Sedge*
Carex scabrata Sedge
Corydalis sempervirens Pale Corydalis
Cypripedium acaule Pink Lady's Slipper*
***Cypripedium parviflorum var. pubes-
  cens*** Large-flowered Yellow Lady's
  Slipper*
Hydrastis canadensis Goldenseal*
Hypericum buckleii Blue Ridge St.
  Johnswort
Isotria medeoloides Small Whorled
  Pogonia†
Juglans cinerea Butternut (nut-bearing
  only)
Juncus gymnocarpus Naked-fruit Rush
Leiophyllum buxifolium Sand-myrtle
Lonicera dioica Limber Honeysuckle
Lysimachia terrestris Bog Candles
Melanthium latifolium Broadleaf
  Bunchflower
Menziesia pilosa Minniebush
Muhlenbergia sobolifera Sprouting
  Muhly
Panax quinquefolius American Ginseng

Pedicularis lanceolata Swamp Lousewort

Penstemon smallii Small's Beardtongue

Platanthera flava var. herbiola Leafy Southern Tubercled Orchid

Platanthera psycodes Small Purple-fringe Orchid

Prunus pensylvanica Fire Cherry

Pycnanthemum curvipes Stone Mountain-mint

Pycnanthemum virginianum Virginia Mountain-mint

Sambucus racemosa ssp. pubens Red Elderberry

Sarracenia oreophila Green Pitcherplant†

Sibbaldiopsis tridentata Three-tooth Cinquefoil*

Streptopus roseus Rosy Twisted Stalk

Trillium simile Sweet White Trillium

Vaccinium erythrocarpum Bearberry

Veratrum viride American False Hellebore

Viburnum lantanoides Witch-hobble

TREUTLEN

Marshallia ramosa Pineland Barbara Buttons*

Penstemon dissectus Grit Beardtongue*

Sarracenia flava Yellow Flytrap*

Scutellaria ocmulgee Ocmulgee Skullcap*

Sideroxylon sp. I Ohoopee Bumelia

Sporobolus teretifolius Wire-leaf Dropseed

TROUP

Iris brevicaulis Lamance Iris

Schisandra glabra Bay Starvine*

TURNER

Balduina atropurpurea Purple Honeycomb Head*

Elliottia racemosa Georgia Plume*

Lophiola aurea Goldcrest

Macranthera flammea Flame Flower

Oxypolis ternata Savanna Cowbane

Penstemon dissectus Grit Beardtongue*

Platanthera integra Yellow Fringeless Orchid

Rhynchospora solitaria Autumn Beakrush

Sarracenia flava Yellow Flytrap*

Sarracenia minor Hooded Pitcherplant*

Sarracenia psittacina Parrot Pitcherplant*

Sporobolus teretifolius Wire-leaf Dropseed

Xyris drummondii Drummond Yellow-eyed Grass

TWIGGS

Nestronia umbellula Indian Olive*

Trillium reliquum Relict Trillium†

UNION

Acer spicatum Mountain Maple

Agastache scrophulariifolia Purple Giant Hyssop

Amelanchier sanguina Roundleaf Serviceberry

Aralia nudicaulis Wild Sarsaparilla

Aster phlogifolius Phlox-leaved Aster

Calystegia catesbeiana ssp. sericata Silky Bindweed

Campanula aparinoides Marsh Bellflower

Carex appalachca Appalachian Sedge

Carex brunnescens Sedge

Carex manhartii Manhart Sedge*

Carex platyphylla Broadleaf Sedge

Carex purpurifera Purple Sedge*

Carex scabrata Sedge

Celastrus scandens Bittersweet

Clintonia borealis Yellow Bead-lily

Coreopsis latifolia Broadleaf Tickseed

Corydalis sempervirens Pale Corydalis

Cypripedium acaule Pink Lady's Slipper*

Cypripedium parviflorum var. pubescens Large-flowered Yellow Lady's Slipper*

Dicentra canadensis Squirrel-corn

Frullania appalachiana A Liverwort

Gentianopsis crinita Fringed Gentian*

Hydrastis canadensis Goldenseal*

Hypericum buckleii Blue Ridge St. Johnswort

Isotria medeoloides Small Whorled Pogonia†

Juglans cinerea Butternut (nut-bearing only)

Juncus gymnocarpus Naked-fruit Rush

Leiophyllum buxifolium Sand-myrtle

Listera smallii Appalachian Twayblade

Lonicera dioica Limber Honeysuckle

Lycopodium clavatum Ground Pine

Lygodium palmatum Climbing Fern

Melanthium latifolium Broadleaf Bunchflower

Menziesia pilosa Minniebush

Panax quinquefolius American Ginseng

Paronychia argyrocoma Silverling

Penstemon smallii Small's Beardtongue

Platanthera peramoena Purple Fringeless Orchid

Platanthera psycodes Small Purple-fringe Orchid

Prunus pensylvanica Fire Cherry

Prunus virginiana Chokecherry

Pycnanthemum curvipes Stone Mountain-mint

Sibbaldiopsis tridentata Three-tooth Cinquefoil*

Silene ovata Mountain Catchfly

Sorbus americana American Mountain-ash

Spiraea alba var. latifolia Broadleaf White Spirea

Spiraea tomentosa Hardhack

Stachys hispida Hispid Hedge-nettle

Thalictrum coriaceum Leatherleaf Meadowrue

Trientalis borealis Northern Starflower*

Trillium simile Sweet White Trillium

Triosteum aurantiacum Wild Coffee

Vaccinium erythrocarpum Bearberry

Veratrum viride American False Hellebore

UPSON

Hymenocallis coronaria Shoals Spiderlily*

Silene polypetala Fringed Campion†

Trillium reliquum Relict Trillium†

Waldsteinia lobata Piedmont Barren Strawberry*

WALKER

Aesculus glabra Ohio Buckeye

Agalinis decemloba Purple Foxglove

Aster ericoides Heath Aster

Aster phlogifolius Phlox-leaved Aster

Aster pradealtus Willow-leaf Aster

Astranthium integrifolium Wild Daisy

Baptisia australis var. aberrans Glade Blue Indigo

Buchnera americana Bluehearts

Camassia scilloides Wild Hyacinth

Carex albursina White Bear Lake Sedge

Carex platyphylla Broadleaf Sedge

Carex purpurifera Purple Sedge*

Carex stricta Tussock Sedge

Carya laciniosa Shellbark Hickory

Cheilanthes alabamensis Alabama Lipfern

Cotinus obovatus American Smoketree

Crataegus triflora Three-flower Hawthorn

Cypripedium acaule Pink Lady's Slipper*

Cystopteris tennesseensis Tennessee Fragile Fern

Balea gattingeri Gattinger Prairie Clover

Dasistoma macrophylla Mullein
  Foxglove

Desmodium ochroleucum Creamflower
  Tick-trefoil

Diarrhena americana American
  Dropseed

Dryopteris celsa Log Fern

Erigenia bulbosa Harbinger-of-spring

Fothergilla major Mountain Witch-alder

Fraxinus quadrangulata Blue Ash

Hydrastis canadensis Goldenseal*

Hypericum dolabriforme Glade St.
  Johnswort

Jeffersonia diphylla Twinleaf*

Juncus filipendulus Texas Plains Rush

Juncus gymnocarpus Naked-fruit Rush

Leavenworthia exigua var. exigua
  Gladecress*

Leavenworthia uniflora Gladecress

Lilium philadephicum Wood Lily

Lithospermum latifolium Broadleaf
  Gromwell

Lygodium palmatum Climbing Fern

Lysimachia fraseri Fraser Loosestrife*

Matelea obliqua Limerock Milkvine

Melanthium woodii Ozark Bunchflower*

Mertensia virginica Virginia Bluebells

Muhlenbergia sobolifera Sprouting
  Muhly

Neviusia alabamensis Alabama Snow-
  wreath*

Onosmodium molle ssp. occidentale
  Marble-seed

Ophioglossum engelmannii Limestone
  Adder-tongue Fern

Panax quinquefolius American Ginseng

Paronychia argyrocoma Silverling

Phacelia purshii Miami-mist

Philadelphus pubenscens Hairy
  Mockorange

Phlox amplifolia Broadleaf Phlox

Polymnia laevigata Tennessee Leafcup

Potamogeton amplifolius Bigleaf
  Pondweed

Ribes curvatum Granite Gooseberry

Sabatia capitata Cumberland Rose
  Gentian*

Scutellaria montana Large-flowered
  Skullcap†

Silene rotundifolia Roundleaf Catchfly

Spiraea virginiana Virginia Spirea†

Stachys nuttallii Nuttall's Hedge-nettle

Stylophorum diphyllum Celandine Poppy

Symphyotrichum sericeum Silky Aster

Trichomanes boschianum Appalachian
  Filmy Fern

Trichomanes petersii Dwarf Filmy Fern

Trillium flexipes Bent Trillium

Trillium lancifolium Lanceleaf Trillium

Trillium sulcatum Barksdale Trillium

Ulmus serotina September Elm

Virburnum bracteatum Limerock
  Arrowwood*

Woodsia scopulina ssp. appalachiana
  Appalachian Cliff Fern

WALTON

Allium speculae Flatrock Onion*

Amphianthus pusillus Pool Sprite†

Amsonia ludoviciana Lousiana Blue Star

Anemone berlandieri Glade Windflower

Aster avitus Alexander Rock Aster

Draba aprica Open-ground Whitlow-
  grass*

Eleocharis wolfii Spikerush

Eriocaulon koernickianum Dwarf
  Pipewort

Fimbristylis brevivaginata Flatrock
  Fimbry

Pilularia americana American Pillwort

Sedum pusillum Granite Stonecrop*

Trepocarpus aesthusae Trepocarpus

WARE

Agalinis aphylla Scale-leaf Purple Foxglove

Agalinis divaricata Pineland Purple Foxglove

Agalinis filicaulis Spindly Purple Foxglove

Epidendrum conopseum Green-fly Orchid*

Fuirena scirpoidea Southern Umbrella-sedge

Hartwrightia floridana Hartwrightia*

Lobelia boykinii Boykin Lobelia

Peltandra sagittifolia Arrow Arum

Rhynchospora alba Northern White Beaksedge

Sarracenia flava Yellow Flytrap*

Sarracenia minor Hooded Pitcherplant*

Sarracenia psittacina Parrot Pitcherplant*

Scirpus etuberculatus Canby's Club-rush

Scutellaria arenicola Sandhill Skullcap

WARREN

Sedum pusillum Granite Stonecrop*

Silene caroliniana Carolina Pink

WASHINGTON

Astragalus michauxii Sandhill Milkvetch

Cuscuta harperi Harper Dodder*

Marshallia ramosa Pineland Barbara Buttons*

Pilularia americana American Pillwort

Schisandra glabra Bay Starvine*

Stewartia malacodendron Silky Camellia*

WAYNE

Asimina reticulata Netleaf Pawpaw

Baptisia arachnifera Hairy Rattleweed†

Epidendrum conopseum Green-fly Orchid*

Fothergilla gardenii Dwarf Witch-alder*

Liatris pauchiflora Few-flower Gay-feather

Litsea aestivalis Pondspice*

Matelea alabamensis Alabama Milkvine*

Peltandra sagittifolia Arrow Arum

Phaseolus polystachios var. sinuatus Trailing Bean-vine

Plantago sparsiflora Pineland Plantain

Quercus austrina Bluff White Oak

Quercus chapmanii Chapman Oak

Rhexia nuttallii Nuttall Meadowbeauty

Sarracenia flava Yellow Flytrap*

Sarracenia minor Hooded Pitcherplant*

WEBSTER

Hexastylis shuttleworthii var. harperi Harper Heartleaf*

Quercus arkansana Arkansas Oak

Rudbeckia auriculata Swamp Black-eyed Susan

WHEELER

Andropogon mohrii Bog Bluestem

Ceratiola ericoides Rosemary*

Elliottia racemosa Georgia Plume

Lindera melissifolia Pondberry†

Litsea aestivalis Pondspice*

Marshallia ramosa Pineland Barbara Buttons*

Nestronia umbellula Indian Olive*

Penstemon dissectus Grit Beardtongue*

Quercus sinuata Durand Oak

Sarracenia flava Yellow Flytrap*

Sarracenia minor Hooded Pitcherplant*
Sarracenia rubra Sweet Pitcherplant†
Scutellaria mellichampii Skullcap
Scutellaria ocmulgee Ocmulgee
Skullcap*
Sideroxylon sp. I Ohoopee Bumelia
Sporobolus teretifolius Wire-leaf
Dropseed
Tradescantia roseolens Rosy Spiderwort

WHITE

Carex biltmoreana Biltmore Sedge*
Carex manhartii Manhart Sedge*
Comptonia peregrine Sweet-fern
Cypripedium acaule Pink Lady's Slipper*
Cypipedium parviflorum var. pubescens Large-flowered Yellow Lady's
Slipper*
Hypnum cupressiforme var. filiforme A
Moss
Juglans cinerea Butternut (nut-bearing
only)
Juncus gymnocarpus Naked-fruit Rush
Lygodium palmatum Climbing Fern
Melantium latifolium Broadleaf
Bunchflower
Menziesia pilosa Minniebush
Panax quinquefolius American Ginseng
Panax trifolius Dwarf Ginseng
Rhus typhina Florida Torreya
Triosteum aurantiacum Wild Coffee

WHITFIELD

Chaerophyllum procumbens
Spreading Chervil
Cypripedium acaule Pink Lady's Slipper*
Cypripedium parviflorum var. pubescens Large-flowered Yellow Lady's
Slipper*
Hydrophyllum macrophyllum Largeleaf
Waterleaf

Isoetes appalachiana Bigspore
Engelmann's Quillwort
Lsimachia fraseri Fraser Loosestrife*
Mertensia virginica Virginia Bluebells
Panax quinquefolius American Ginseng
Phlox amplifolia Broadleaf Phlox
Polemonium reptans Jacob's ladder
Scutellaria montana Large-flowered
Skullcap†
Trillium lancifolium Lanceleaf Trillium
Trillium pusillum Least Trillium
Xyris tennesseensis Tennessee Yellow-
eyed Grass†

WILCOX

Armoracia lacustris Lake-cress
Marshallia ramosa Pineland Barbara
Buttons*
Oldenlandia boscii Bluets
Sarracenia flava Yellow Flytrap*
Sarracenia minor Hooded Pitcherplant*
Sarracenia psittacina Parrot Pitcherplant
Scutellaria ocmulgee Ocmulgee
Skullcap*
Sideroxylon thornei Swamp Buckthorn*
Spermacoce glabra Smooth Buttonweed

WILKES

Amorpha schwerinii Schwerin
Indigo-bush
Draba aprica Open-ground Whitlow-
grass*
Hymenocallis coronaria Shoals
Spiderlily*
Nestronia umbellula Indian Olive*
Quercus oglethorpensis Oglethorpe Oak*
Sedum pusillum Granite Stonecrop*

WILKINSON

Stewartia malacondendron Silky Camellia*

Trillium reliquum Relict Trillium†

Waldsteinia lobata Piedmont Barren Strawberry*

WORTH

Angelica dentate Sandhill Angelica

Balduina atropurpurea Purple Honeycomb Head*

Drosera tracyi Tracy's Dew-threads

Elyonurus tripsacoides Pan-american Balsamscale

Lindera melissifolia Pondberry†

Lobelia boykini Boykin Lobelia

Macranthera flammea Flame Flower

Marshallia ramosa Pineland Barbara Buttons*

Oxypolis ternata Savanna Cowbane

Penstemon dissectus Grit Beardtongue*

Platanthera nivea Snowy Orchid

Pteroglossaspis ecristata Wild Coco

Sarracenia flava Yellow Flytrap*

Sarracenia minor Hooded Pitcherplant*

Sarracenia psittacina Parrot Pitcherplant*

Sideroxylon thornei Swamp Buckthorn*

Sporobolus teretifolius Wire-leaf Dropseed

Stokesia laevis Stokes Aster

Thalictrum cooleyi Cooley Meadowrue†

Xyris scabrifolia Harper Yellow-eyed Grass

AS THE VINE CONSUMES:
A BRIEF OVERVIEW OF KUDZU AND COGONGRASS

"That Kudzu Vine"
sung to the tune of "I Walk the Line" by Johnny Cash
by Merry & Pippin (Kathie Weigel and Luke Cossins)

I keep a close watch on that farm of mine
Because it's crept wide over Caroline
It ate my fence and half of my combine
It's here to dine, that kudzu vine

I find that early Sunday morning my poor cow
It fell asleep alone next to my ol' plow
Yes it's sad it's all green and shaggy now
It's here to dine, that kudzu vine

To keep me quite from harm of stray vine blight
I close my windows tight both day and night
Plant voracious has shown its appetite
It's here to dine, that kudzu vine

I've spent a way too much on herbicide
'Cus it will be alive past when I've died
Boo hoo, I know my garden fell to kudzucide
It's here to dine, that kudzu vine

I keep a close watch on that farm of mine
I watch my rice, rye, oats, corn in decline
And now it's entwined a full sty of swine
It came to dine, that kudzu vine

THE HISTORY OF KUDZU [9]

2699 BC Chon-nong, emperor of China, composed a catalog of Chinese herbs. Supposedly, kudzu was listed in the catalog.

200 BC   The earliest verifiable records show that kudzu was used as an herbal medicine.

1700s Kudzu was imported into Japan from China.

1876 Kudzu was first introduced into the United States at the Philadelphia Centennial Exposition in the Japanese Pavilion.

1884 Kudzu was introduced to the South through the exhibit at the Japanese Pavilion at the New Orleans Exposition.

1900 Kudzu is planted around porches throughout the South for its fragrant flowers, its ability to provide shade, and its ability to climb up the porch.

1902 Botanist David Fairchild observed that kudzu can be invasive.

1902 Florida farmers Charles and Lillie Pleas devoted fifty years of their lives to promoting the benefits of kudzu as an agricultural and soil-saving plant. After his death, a bronze plaque was erected near Mr. Pleas's agricultural center, announcing "Kudzu Was Developed Here."

1935 US Soil Conservation research affirmed kudzu's effectiveness in erosion control, soil improvements, and cattle feed. The US Government then offered assistance payments of up to eight dollars for each acre of kudzu planted.

1938 David Fairchild's warning about the invasiveness of kudzu was published.

1940 The Soil Erosion Service, established by Congress in 1933 (later renamed the Soil Conservation Service), produced the 73,000,000th kudzu seedling and employed thousands of Civilian Conservation Corps workers to plant them along highways and ditches.

1943 The Kudzu Club of America was formed in Atlanta by Channing Cope.

1953 USDA removed kudzu from its list of recommended cover crops.

1960 Kudzu research focus shifted from propagation to eradication.

1966 Dr. Wing-Ming Keung of Harvard University Medical School said basic research on kudzu as a treatment for alcoholism had produced promising results.

1970 USDA declared kudzu a weed.

1979 Union, South Carolina, had its first kudzu festival, including a beauty pageant, sporting events, and kudzu craft and cooking demonstrations.

1981 The *Kudzu* comic strip by Doug Marlette began. It is now syndicated.

1982 Chattanooga, Tennessee, had its first Kudzu Ball.

1985 Diane and Matt Hoots (founders of Krazy Kudzu Product, Ltd.) made their first kudzu baskets.

1994 Krazy Kudzu Products, Ltd. was formed to market kudzu products.

1994 Georgia State Representative Tom Buck introduced a bill to make it a misdemeanor to have kudzu growing from one's property onto another person's property.

1996 Dalton, Georgia, held its first annual kudzu festival.

1997 Congress proclaimed kudzu a noxious weed.

1999 Stone Mountain, Georgia, held its first kudzu festival.

Kudzu (*Pueraria lobata*) is a native of Japan that was brought to the United States in 1876 via the Philadelphia Centennial Exposition. Not long afterward, the New Orleans Expedition made it an overgrowing part of the South. Although the plant has always been troublesome, farmers during the Great Depression were paid an impressive eight dollars per acre to plant kudzu, which was believed to help prevent erosion. Kudzu, a perennial vine and member of the bean family, covers more than 7,000,000 acres in the Southeast. In early summer, its peak growing season, kudzu grows at the rate of 1 foot each day. No matter how diverse the growing conditions, kudzu can find a way to flourish. In fact, it takes more than ten years to kill a well-established kudzu patch. It is the single worst threat to native plants in Georgia, mostly due to over-crowding and shading the landscape. Kudzu literally chokes everything in its path. It is used in a wide variety of projects, ranging from medicinal to decorative and from teas to alcoholism therapy, in hopes of finding more ways to combat its overgrowth.

Cogongrass, hailed as the "new kudzu," is a highly invasive perennial weed with upright shoots measuring 2–4 feet high. It is spread via wind-blown seeds. The leaf margins have silica crystals and silvery hairless blades. Hardy cogongrass, found in any ecosystem, tolerates shade and drought. It was introduced into the United States as a packing material and, like kudzu, studied as an erosion crop. Though relatively new to Georgia, it is still on a watch list. Researchers in Florida, Alabama, and Mississippi are seeking viable control options for cogongrass. Due to its extreme dense cover created by a mat of thatch and leaves, cogongrass can displace ground nesting species. It is nearly impossible for other plants to exist or for animals to live in areas with cogongrass.

THE BOTANICAL SIGNIFICANCE OF FLOYD COUNTY, GEORGIA

Floyd County contains some of the most diverse botany in the United States. In 1899, noted botanist Chauncey D. Beadle came to Rome from North Carolina's Biltmore Herbarium and discovered several new hawthorns in the area. Included in these discoveries were the first specimens of *Crataegus regalis* and *Crataegus mohri*.

Additional botanical finds were made by Charles Boyton, another Biltmore Herbarium collector, who discovered Georgia's first *Ulmus serotina* (September elm) near Rome. However, perhaps the most celebrated visit during that era was from John Muir. Muir has been called "Father of National Parks" and was the most famous of conservationists.

Floyd County Stats
Population per 2000 census – 90,565
Rainfall yearly average – 47 inches
Winter temperature average – 54F
Summer temperature average – 79F

Floyd County Protected Wildflowers
Arabis georgiana (Georgia Rockcress)
Carex purpurifera (Purple Sedge)
Clematis socialis (Alabama Leather Flower)
Cypripedium acaule (Pink Lady's Slipper)
Cypripedium calceolus (Yellow Lady's Slipper)
Helianthus verticillatus (Whorled Sunflower)
Marshallia mohrii (Coosa Barbara Buttons)
Sabatia capitata (Cumberland Rose Gentian)
Scutellaria montana (Large-flowered Skullcap)
Silene regia (Royal Catchfly)
Spiranthes magnicamporum (Great Plains Ladies-tresses)
Thalictrum debile (Trailling Meadow-rue)
Viburnum bracteatum (Limerock Arrowwood)
Xyris tennesseensis (Tennessee Yellow-eyed Grass)

Accompanied by William Canby and Charles Sargeant, he ventured throughout Rome and the Coosa River and discovered nearly six dozen trees that were new to the area.

Many gardeners who come to Rome realize that the soil is rich, the weather is nearly tropic, and there are few challenges (despite the famous Georgia drought). With its moderate temperature range, respectable rainfall amounts, and the heightened conservation efforts of its people, Rome (the city incorporating Floyd County) is privy to three prime botanical havens—Marshall Forest, Black's Bluff, and the Floyd College Wetlands.

Marshall Forest

This National Natural Landmark encompasses 311 acres, 75 of which are in Floyd County, and has more than 300 species of plant life in its plain. Besides being the only virgin forest in a city's limits, it is also the only virgin forest from Pennsylvania to Alabama (an area known as the "Ridge and Valley Province"). The forest offers five nature trails on which people can identify the plant life through simple identifcation tags and information stations. One of the trails, the Big Pine Braille Trail, can be walked in only thirty minutes and is self-guided. Many of its signs are written in both Braille and English. In 1977, Boy Scout Troup No. 34, the Four Seasons Garden Club in Rome, and students at Shorter College cleared this particular trail

Marshall Forest a favorite of naturalists. An ever-growing site of 55 tree species and 250 other plant species, it is protected by the Nature Conservatory. To schedule a tour of the area, contact Dr. Mark Knauss at Friends of Marshall Forest, 315 Shorter Ave, Rome, GA 30165, or call (706) 291-2121.

Black's Bluff

This 500 million-year-old 130-acre preserve is the growing site of two of Georgia's finest species—*Scutellaria montana* (Large-flowered Skullcap)

and *Viburnum bracteatum* (Limerock Arrowwood). The bluff offers diverse flora, from northern plants to native wildflowers due to the alkalinity of its rich limestone. It was here that botanists from the Biltmore Estates came to observe the richness of the region's flora. Black's Bluff is one of only two different preserves in Georgia open to the public every day of the week. It is protected by the Nature Conservatory.

Floyd College Wetlands

This 20-acre haven is home to meadows, forests, streams, a cattail marshland, and a willow swamp. The Floyd College Wetlands' 1,200-foot boardwalk makes it accessible to its many visitors. Touring the wetlands via the boardwalk allows one to observe the diverse ecosystem without getting wet. Along the path are twelve different viewing areas that highlight key features. Other than this raised boardwalk, which trails through the preserve, the 20 flowing acres are completely undisturbed, allowing plant life to filter the water and produce nearly three times the biomass of other ecosystems. Students can learn about biodiversity, and people can also come to the preserve as a natural getaway.

Take a virtual tour of these wetlands at
http://www.floyd.edu/swamp/index.htm.

LAYING THE GROUNDWORK

A Soil, Mulch, and Compost Guide

Soil Particle Size
Sand
Very coarse: 1.0–2.0 mm
Coarse: .50–1.0 mm
Medium: .25–.50 mm
Fine: .10–.25 mm
Very fine: .05–.10 mm

Silt: .002–.05 mm

Clay: less than .002mm

Soil Composition
Sandy soils: more than 35 percent sand, less than 15 percent silt and clay

Coarse sand: more than 35 percent very coarse or coarse sand, less than 50 percent fine or very fine sand

Medium sand: more than 35 percent coarse and medium sand, less than 50 percent fine or very fine sand

Fine sand: more than 50 percent fine or very fine sand

Very fine sand: more than 50 percent very fine sand

Loam soils: less than 20 percent clay, 30–50 percent silt, 30–50 percent sand

Sandy loam: 20–50 percent silt and clay

Coarse sandy loam: more than 45 percent very coarse and coarse sand

Medium sandy loam: more than 25 percent very coarse or coarse sand and medium sand, less than 35 percent very fine sand

Fine sandy loam: more than 50 percent fine, less than 25 percent very coarse or coarse sand and medium sand

Very fine sandy loam: more than 35 percent very fine sand

Silt loam: less than 20 percent clay, more than 50 percent silt

Clay loam: 20–30 percent clay

Sandy clay loam: less than 30 percent silt, 50–80 percent sandy, 20–30 percent clay

Silty clay loam: 20–50 percent silt, 20–50 percent sand, 20–30 percent clay

Clay soils: more than 30 percent clay, less than 50 percent silt, less than 50 percent sand

Sandy clay: 30–50 percent clay, less than 20 percent silt, 50–70 percent sand

Silty clay: 30–50 percent clay, 50–70 percent silt, less than 20 percent sand

Testing Your Soil Type

You can have your soil accurately tested, but the following methods are easy ways to get a quick idea of your soil type. Two days after rainfall, collect a sample of earth the size of a golf ball and squeeze it. If the earth feels gritty, it is sandy soil; if smooth, it is silty; and if slippery, it is clay. Next, open your hand. If the earth does not hold together, it is sandy soil; if it crumbles slowly, it is loamy; and if it sticks together, it is clay.

Potting Soil Recipes

(A) 1 part perlite, 1 part peat moss, 1 part vermiculite

(B) 1 part garden soil, 1 part peat moss, 1 part builder's sand

(C) 1 part soil, 1 part milled sphagnum moss, 1 part peat moss

(D) 1 part peat moss, 1 part sieved compost

(E) 2 parts soil, 1 part compost, 1 part perlite

John Innes Compost (Famous British mix): 7 parts composted loam, 3 parts peat moss, 2 parts coarse sand, 1 1/2 parts ground limestone, 8 1/2 parts fertilizer (2 parts hoof and horn meal, 2 parts super phosphate, 1 part sulfate of potash) *or* 12 parts 5–10–10 fertilizer.

Mulch Guide

Summer mulching helps attract worms, slow water evaporation and weed growth, and nourish the soil and keep it moist. Winter mulching mostly protects the soil from deep freezing and keeps roots from becoming damaged from too much freezing/thawing cycles. The following is a guide for the different types of mulches.

Bark chips: Long lasting but expensive. Larger pieces last longer. Spread bark chips 2 inches deep, and add nitrogen to the soil before you mulch.

Shredded bark: Long lasting but expensive. Spread 3 inches deep, and add nitrogen to the soil before you mulch.

Buckwheat hulls: Last approximately two years. Spread 2 inches deep.

Cocoa bean hulls: Short–lived chocolate smell. Expensive. Good for formal gardens. Spread 2 inches deep.

Compost: Nourishing mulch, but not a weed barrier. Spread 1–2 inches deep.

Ground corncobs: Inexpensive. Spread 3–4 inches deep, and add nitrogen to the soil before you mulch.

Cottonseed hulls: Good weed suppressor. Spread 3–4 inches deep, and add nitrogen to the soil before you mulch.

Hay/Straw: Lightweight. Will compact in the garden over time. Hay may contain weed seeds; most straw is free of such seeds. Spread 4–6 deep inches in summer; 8–12 inches in winter.

Shredded leaves: Weed suppressor. Good winter mulch. Used in naturalistic woodland gardens. Spread 2–3 deep inches in summer; 6–8 in winter.

Peanut hulls: Lightweight. Spread 2–3 deep inches deep.

Pine needles: Lightweight and long lasting. Use around acid-loving plants like azaleas. Spread 3–4 inches deep.

Sawdust: Cheap, acidic mulch. Spread 2–3 inches deep, and add nitrogen to the soil before mulching.

Stone, gravel, marble chips: Use over black plastic as a weed suppressor. Best around trees and shrubs. Spread 2–3 inches deep.

Wood chips: Long lasting, but decomposes faster than bark. Spread 2–3 inches deep, and add nitrogen to the soil before you mulch.

HELPFUL RESOURCES FOR GARDENERS

The following list of organizations can help you plan, plant, and maintain a native garden. [10]

The Bugwood Network and ForestryImages.org
Home page:
http://www.forestryimages.org/
Chuck Bargeron
P.O. Box 748
300 H. H. Tift Building CPES
The University of Georgia
Tifton, GA 31793
Ph: 229-386-3298

Georgia Botanical Society
Home page: http://www.gabotsoc.org
E-mail address: members@gabotsoc.org
320 Ashton Drive
Athens, GA 30606-1622
Ph: 706-353-8222

Georgia Department of Natural Resources
Wildlife Resources Division
Georgia Natural Heritage Program
Home page: http://georgiawildlife.com
2117 US Hwy 278 SE
Social Circle, GA 30025-4714
Ph: 770-918-6411

Georgia Native Plant Society
Home page: http://www.gnps.org
E-mail address: webmaster@gnps.org
P.O. Box 422085
Atlanta, GA 30342-2085
Ph: 770-343-6000

Georgia Perennial Plant Association
Home page:
http://www.mindspring.com/~guzy/
P.O. Box 13425
Atlanta, GA 30324-0425
Ph: 404-237-8071

Georgia Southern Botanical Garden
Home page:
http://www2.gasou.edu/garden/
P.O. Box 8039
Statesboro, GA 30460

Georgia Wildlife Federation
Home page: http://www.gwf.org
E-mail address: webmaster@gwf.org
11600 Hazelbrand Road
Covington, GA 30014
Ph: 770-787-7887
Fax: 770-787-9229

Invaders Database System
Home page: http://invader.dbs.umt.edu
Peter Rice
Division of Biological Sciences
University of Montana
Missoula, MT 59812
Ph: 406-243-2671

The State Botanical Garden of Georgia
Home page: http://www.uga.edu/~bot-garden/home2.html
2450 South Milledge Avenue
Athens, GA 30605
Ph: 706-542-1244

University of Georgia Trial Gardens
Home page: http://ugatrial.hort.uga.edu
Dr. Allan Armitage
1111 Plant Sciences Building
Department of Horticulture
University of Georgia
Athens, GA 30602
Ph: 706-542-2471
Fax: 706-542-2464

RECOMMENDED READING

Chaplin, Lois. *The Southern Gardener's Book of Lists: The Best Plants for All Your Needs, Wants, and Whims.* Taylor Publishing Company, February 1994. ISBN 0878338446.

Foote, Leonard, and Samuel Jones, Jr. *Native Shrubs and Woody Vines of the Southeast: Landscaping Uses and Identification.* Timber Press, Inc., March 1998. ISBN 0881924164.

Glasener, Erica, and Walter Reeves. *Flowers for Georgia: 50 Great Plants for Georgia Gardens.* Cool Springs Press, December 2003. ISBN 1591860806.

———. *Month-by-Month Gardening in Georgia.* Cool Springs Press, March 2001. ISBN 1888608277.

Hastings, Don, and Steve Hastings. *Don Hastings' Month-by-Month Gardening in the South: What to Do and When to Do It.* Longstreet Press, Inc., December 1998. ISBN 1563525518.

Midgley, Jan. *Southeastern Wildflowers: Your Complete Guide to Plant Communities, Identification, Culture, Propagation and Traditional Uses.* Crane Hill Publishers, August 1999. ISBN 1575871068.

Reeves, Walter, and Erica Glasener. *Georgia Gardener's Guide.* Cool Springs Press, January 2004. ISBN 159186044X.

Rushing, Felder. *Tough Plants for Southern Gardens.* Cool Springs Press, May 2003. ISBN 1591860024.

Wasowski, Sally, and Andy Wasowski. *Gardening with Native Plants of the South.* Taylor Publishing Company, February 1994. ISBN 0878338020.

Winter, Norman. *Tough-as-Nails Flowers for the South.* Norman Winter. University Press of Mississippi, March 2003. ISBN 1578065445.

Xeriscape Plant Guide: 100 Water-Wise Plants for Gardens and Landscapes. Fulcrum Publishing, March 1999. ISBN 1555912532.

WHERE TO BUY GEORGIA NATIVE PLANTS: A STORE GUIDE[11]

Country Keepsakes Garden Center and Pond Headquarters
6545 Hwy. 92
Acworth GA 30102
770-516-1777

Perennial Grace Nursery, Inc.
14395 Birmingham Hwy.
Alpharetta GA 30004
770-569-1929

Native Sun, Inc.
395 Bob Holman Rd.
Athens GA 30607
706-227-2811

Ashe Simpson Garden Center
4961 Peachtree Industrial Blvd.
Atlanta GA 30341
770-458-3224

Habersham Gardens
2067 Manchester St.
Atlanta GA 30324
404-873-2484

Hastings
3920 Peachtree Rd.
Atlanta GA 30319
404-869-7447

Picadilly Farms
1971 Whipporwill Rd.
Bishop GA 30621
706-769-6516

Blue Creek Nursery
392 Hunting Hills Dr.
Cleveland GA 30528-3574
706-865-2849

Lost Mountain Nursery
824 Poplar Springs Rd.
Dallas GA 30157
770-427-5583

Melton's Nursery
1741 Bobo Rd.
Dallas GA 30132
770-289-2031

Eco-Gardens
PO Box 1227
Decatur GA 30031
404-294-6468

Georgia Perimeter Botanical Garden
3251 Panthersville Rd.
Decatur GA 30024
404-244-5001

Bannister Creek Nursery
3769 Rogers Bridge Rd.
Duluth GA 30097
770-497-9905
www.bannistercreek.com

Passion Flower Farms
1405 Womack Ave.
East Point GA 30344-1630
404-767-2273
www.passionflowerfarms.com

Turnipseed Nursery Farms
685 South Glynn St. Hwy. 85
Fayetteville GA 30214
770-460-8534

Kinzer Nurseries, LLC
219 Wren Rd.
Jasper GA 30143
706-253-3676
www.kinzernurseries.com

GardenSmith Greenhouse
231 Hogan Mill Rd.
Jefferson GA 30549
706-367-9047

Walker Nursery Farms
2024 Walt Stephens Rd.
Jonesboro GA 30236
770-471-6011
www.walkernursery.com

Goodness Grows
PO Box 311
Lexington GA 30648-0311
706-743-5055

Bittersweet Gardens
667 Longwood Ct.
Marietta GA 30008-3756
678-354-6394

Chattahoochee Home and Garden
4773 Lower Roswell Rd.
Marietta GA 30068
770-977-0981

Kelli Green Greenhouse and Nursery
2514 Shallowford Rd.
Marietta GA 30066
770-928-1190

Southeastern Wholesale Nursery, Inc.
1556 West Oak Dr.
Marietta GA 30062
770-590-3160

Land Arts, Inc.
809 North Broad St.
Monroe GA 30656
770-267-4500

Wilkerson Mill Gardens
9595 Wilkerson Mill Rd.
Palmetto GA 30268
770-463-2400
www.hydrangea.com

Lazy K Nursery, Inc.
—Garden Delights
US Hwy. 27
Pine Mountain GA 31822
706-663-7964

The Green Plant Market, Inc.
2870 GA Hwy. 85
Senoia GA 30276
770-599-8210
www.wegrowit.com

Hall's Flower Shops and Garden Center
5706 Memorial Dr.
Stone Mountain GA 30083
404-292-8446

Thyme after Thyme
550 Athens Rd.
Winterville GA 30683-1535
706-742-7149

Autumn Hill Nursery
4256 Earney Rd.
Woodstock GA 30188
770-442-3901
www.autumnhillnursery.com

Buck Jones Nursery
7470 Hickory Flat Hwy.
Woodstock GA 30188
770-345-5506
www.buckjones.com

Indigo Growers
10138 Main St.
Woodstock GA 30188
770-924-4494

Lady's Slipper Rare Plant Nursery
7418 Hickory Flat Hwy. 140
Woodstock GA 30188
770-345-2998

Mann's Greenhouse
4950 Hickory Rd.
Woodstock GA 30188
770-345-2300

Twin Branch Nursery
1169 Wiley Bridge Rd.
Woodstock GA 30188
770-926-8566

NOTES

[1] Find information online at <http://www.gaeppc.org>.

[2] Find information online at <http://www.bugwood.org>.

[3] For original list, please visit <http://invader.dbs.umt.edu>. Last updated April 18, 2000.

[4] For a complete and updated list, see the Georgia DNR website at
   <www.georgiawildlife.com>.

[5] Deadheading is pinching off the dead bloom or seed head.

[6] The umbrel is a type of flowering structure (inflorescence) from which all individual
   flowers rise.

[7] From the Georgia Natural Heritage Program, Nongame Wildlife and Natural Heritage
   Section, Wildlife Resources Division, Georgia Department of Natural Resources, with
   special permission from Greg Krakow, data manager. This data is for known locations
   only. Since large parts of Georgia have not been thoroughly surveyed, many species
   may occur in counties under which they are not listed. The data is correct as of April
   1, 2004. For the latest data and details, please visit <www.georgiawildlife.com>.

[8] A scientific name and description for this new species has not been officially published.
   The abbreviation "sp" indicates that the plant is still in the process of being classified.

[9] By Krazy Kudzu Products, Ltd. See <www.krazykudzu.com>.

[10] List current as of April 24, 2005. Websites, phone numbers, and addresses may change.

[11] Arranged alphabetically by city.

PHOTO CREDITS

Jennifer Anderson @ USDA-NRCS PLANTS Database
Antennaria plantaginifolia, Cardamine concatenata, Asarum canadense , Lysimachia ciliata, Aquilegia canadensis, Arisaema triphyllum, Lobelia siphilitica, Iris versicolor , Claytonia virginica, Podophyllum peltatum, Helenium autumnale, Sisyrinchium angustifolium, Sanguinaria canadensis, Phlox divaricata, Tradescantia virginiana, Solidago, Arabis georgiana, Spartina pectinata, Sorghastrum nutans, Dodecatheon meadia, Dicentra cucullaria, Geranium maculatum, Rubus occidentalis, Symphyotrichum novae-angliae, Actaea alba, Anemonella thalictroides, Cardamine laciniata

Robert H. Mohlenbrock @ USDA-NRCS PLANTS Database / USDA SCS. 1991. Southern wetland flora: Field office guide to plant species. South National Technical Center, Fort Worth, TX.
Mitchella repens, Mikania scandens, Lonicera sempervirens, Eryngium yuccifolium, Wisteria frutescens, Sarracenia minor, Smilacina racemosa, Lonicera japonica, Parthenocissus quinquefolia, Gelsemium sempervirens, Callicarpa americana, Rhododendron canescens, Panicum virgatum, Clematis virginiana, Vaccinium arboretum, Hydrolea ovata, Microstegium vimineum, Rosa carolina

Robert H. Mohlenbrock @ USDA-NRCS PLANTS Database / USDA NRCS. 1995. Northeast wetland flora: Field office guide to plant species. Northeast National Technical Center, Chester, PA.
Mertensia virginica, Gaultheria procumbens, Myosotis scorpioides, Chamaecyparis thyoides, Eupatorium purpureum, Polygonatum biflorum, Phlox maculata, Cypripedium acaule, Cornus florida, Chionanthus virginicus, Campanula aparinoides, Epilobium angustifolium, Hypericum prolificum, Quercus imbricaria, Tsuga canadensis

Robert H. Mohlenbrock @ USDA-NRCS PLANTS Database / USDA SCS. 1989. Midwest wetland flora: Field office illustrated guide to plant species. Midwest National Technical Center, Lincoln, NE.
Amsonia tabernaemontana, Lobelia cardinalis, Boltonia asteroides, Eupatorium coelestinum, Packera aureus, Erigeron pulchellus, Gentianopsis crinita, Hymenocallis caroliniana,

Phlox paniculata, Ilex verticillata, Chasmanthium latifolium, Chelone glabra, Corydalis flavula, Calystegia sepium, Cyperus esculentus, Camassia scilloides, Chaerophyllum prcumbens

L. Glasscock @ USDA-NRCS PLANTS Database / USDA SCS. 1991. Southern wetland flora: Field office guide to plant species. South National Technical Center, Fort Worth, TX.
Schizachyrium scoparium

USDA-NRCS PLANTS Database / Britton, N. L., and A. Brown. 1913. Illustrated flora of the northern states and Canada. Vol. 1
Ulmus serotina, Iris cristata

USDA-NRCS PLANTS Database / Britton, N. L., and A. Brown. 1913. Illustrated flora of the northern states and Canada. Vol. 2
Caulophyllum thalictroides, Sanguisorba canadensis, Fothergilla gardenia, Crataegus iracunda, Pulsatilla patens, Sedum nevii, Litsea aestivalis, Sarracenia purpurea, Crotalaria sagittalis

USDA-NRCS PLANTS Database / Britton, N. L., and A. Brown. 1913. Illustrated flora of the northern states and Canada. Vol. 3
Scutellaria nervosa, Pycnanthemum virginianum

Clarence A. Rechenthin @ USDA-NRCS PLANTS Database
Xanthium, Glandularia canadensis, Cirsium muticum, Silene virginica, Helianthus annuus, Baptisia australis, Robinia hispida, Ratibida columnifera

Larry Allain @ www.USGS.gov
Ligustrum sinense, Imperata cylindrical, Bignonia capreolata, Asclepias tuberose, Campsis radicans, Iris fulva, Liatris spicata, Sarracenia, Albizia julibrissin, Amianthium muscitoxicum, Ipomoea wrightii, Hibiscus coccineus, Spigelia marilandica, Salvia lyrata, Ruellia caroliniensis, Passiflora incarnate, Cirsium carolinianum, Sassafras albidum, Myrica cerifera, Juniperus virginiana. Ilex opaca, Hydrangea quercifolia, Clethra alnifolia, Aralia spinosa, Betula nigra, Nyssa sylvatica, Cercis Canadensis, Cypripedium parviflorum, Erythronium albidum, Magnolia virginiana, Symphyotrichum pretense, Spiranthes magnicamporum, Lilium michauxii, Rubus trivialis, Erythrina herbacea, Morella cerfera, Pinus elliottii, Salix nigra, Daucus pusillus, Scutellaria elliptica, Diodia teres, Ceratiola ericoides, Sapium sebiferum, Crotalaria (sagittalis), Cyperus rotundus, Achillea (millefolium), Buchnera americana, Echinacea purpurea, Magnolia grandiflora, Ilex, glabra

Courtesy of Smithsonian Institution, Dept. of Systematic Biology, Botany @USDA-NRCS PLANTS Database
Convolvulus arvensis

George Pyne @ USDA-NRCS PLANTS Database / USDA SCS. 1991. Southern wetland flora: Field office guide to plant species. South National Technical Center, Fort Worth, TX. *Sarracenia rubram, Sarracenia flava*

Douglas Ladd @ USDA-NRCS PLANTS Database / USDA SCS. 1989. Midwest wetland flora: Field office illustrated guide to plant species. Midwest National Technical Center, Lincoln NE
Silphium perfoliatum

Carl Hunter @ USDA-NRCS PLANTS Database / USDA SCS. 1991. Southern wetland flora: Field office guide to plant species. South National Technical Center, Fort Worth TX
Clematis crispa, Frangula caroliniana, Cardiospermum halicacabum

USDA-NRCS. 2004. The PLANTS Database (http://plants.usda.gov). National Plant Data Center, Baton Rouge, LA 70874-4490 USA
Lindera melissifolia, Hamamelis virginiana, Loblolly bay

William C. Taylor @ USDA-NRCS PLANTS Database / USDA SCS. 1989. Midwest wetland flora: Field office illustrated guide to plant species. Midwest National Technical Center, Lincoln NE
Asclepias purpurascens

Mike Homoya @ USDA-NRCS PLANTS Database / USDA NRCS. 1995. Northeast wetland flora: Field office guide to plant species. Northeast National Technical Center, Chester PA
Cypripedium reginae

Bill Summers @ USDA-NRCS PLANTS Database / USDA SCS. 1991. Southern wetland flora: Field office guide to plant species. South National Technical Center, Fort Worth TX
Eryngium yuccifolium

USDA-NRCS PLANTS Database / Herman, D. E. et al. 1996. North Dakota tree handbook. USDA NRCS ND State Soil Conservation Committee; NDSU Extension and Western Area Power Admin., Bismarck ND
Populus deltoides, Tilia americana

Ed McDowell, GNPS, PO Box 422085, Atlanta, GA 30342-2085
Helianthus verticillatus

Steve Hurst @ USDA-NRCS PLANTS Database
Phyllostachys aurea, Elaeagnus umbellata

INDEX